C000242592

My Three Angels

A Comedy in Three Acts

Sam and Bella Spewack

A SAMUEL FRENCH ACTING EDITION

SAMUEL FRENCH
FOUNDED 1830

SAMUELFRENCH-LONDON.CO.UK
SAMUELFRENCH.COM

FOR AMATEUR PRODUCTION ENQUIRIES

UNITED KINGDOM AND WORLD EXCLUDING NORTH AMERICA

plays@SamuelFrench-London.co.uk

020 7255 4302/01

Each title is subject to availability from Samuel French,

depending upon country of performance.

MY THREE ANGELS

Presented by H. M. Tennent Ltd and George and Alfred Black at the Lyric Theatre, London, on the 12th May 1955 with the following cast of characters—

(in the order of their appearance)

EMILIE DULAY	*Jane Aird*
FELIX DULAY, her husband	*Cyril Luckham*
MADAME PAROLE	*Patience Collier*
MARIE LOUISE DULAY, Felix's daughter	*Elvi Hale*
ALFRED (4707) ⎤	*Nigel Stock*
JULES (6817) ⎬ convicts	*George Rose*
JOSEPH (3011) ⎦	*Ronald Shiner*
GASTON LEMARE	*Hugh Manning*
PAUL CASSAGON, Gaston's nephew	*Peter Barkworth*
SUB-LIEUTENANT ESPOIR, of the French Navy	*Clifford Elkin*

SYNOPSIS OF SCENES

The action of the play passes in the living-room behind Felix Dulay's general store in Cayenne, French Guiana, South America, in the year 1910

ACT I
Late afternoon on Christmas Eve

ACT II
Later that night

ACT III
Christmas morning

MY THREE ANGELS*

ACT I

SCENE—*The living-room behind Felix Dulay's general store in Cayenne, French Guiana, South America. Late afternoon on Christmas Eve, 1910.*
The climate is hot and humid and the room reflects the tropics, but the furniture has obviously been imported from France and bespeaks another world. Most of the walls and ceiling are planks and bamboo, but here and there there are stretches of open lattice work. An arch down R, *hung with a bamboo bead curtain, leads to the kitchen. A slatted door up* R *gives access to the shop. A bell rings when someone enters the shop and this can be heard in the living-room. Across the back is a verandah with a slatted roof, with a view of the tropical garden beyond and a wide expanse of sky in the distance. Two steps between two supporting beams lead up to the verandah. Up* L *is an open archway leading to the family quarters. Below the arch are two slatted doors leading to two guest rooms. These rooms and the archway are on a slightly higher level and to reach them there is a step on to a rostrum which extends some two or three feet on stage. A heavy bamboo pole rises from the rostrum to the ceiling. A red swag border stretches from the top of the pole to above the shop door up* R. *This is enhanced by a lace curtain, gathered in a drape, to a point just below the shop door. A crude ladder can be seen on the verandah, its base just behind the left beam and its top disappearing through a large hole in the slatted verandah roof. There is an oval dining-table* RC *with upright chairs above and* L *of it and an armless easy chair* R *of it. A sideboard stands* R *with occasional chairs above and below it. There is a heavy carved hat-stand above the shop door up* R. *Against the wall above the arch* L *is a bamboo whatnot with some shelves hanging on the wall over it. Below the whatnot is a high-backed wicker armchair with a small circular beaded footstool. Down* R *is a metal-legged occasional table. There are the usual pictures and decorations on the walls, a mirror between the doors of the guest rooms; some antlers and a barometer-thermometer over the table down* R. *There is an oval carpet where the dining-table stands. There is a pile of crates, baskets and boxes in each corner up* R *and* L, *some spilling on to the verandah itself. At night the room is lit by an oil lamp hanging from the ceiling directly over the table and three other oil lamps, one on the sideboard, one on the right beam by the verandah and one on the bamboo pole* LC.
(See the Ground Plan and Photograph of the Scene)

When the CURTAIN *rises, the room is empty and brightly lit by the intense tropical sunshine. The music of a mouth-organ can be heard off.*

---

* N.B. Paragraph 3 on p. ii of this Acting Edition regarding Video-recording and photocopying should be carefully read.

EMILIE (*off; calling*) Felix. Felix.

(EMILIE *and* FELIX DULAY *enter simultaneously,* EMILIE *from the shop up* R *and* FELIX *by the arch up* L. FELIX *carries a small block of wood and a penknife*)

FELIX. Yes, my dear? (*He crosses and stands above the table*)
EMILIE (*moving up* R *of the table*) Would you look after the shop for a little while, dear?
FELIX. Of course, dear. Have you been busy?
EMILIE. No. I haven't seen a customer for about half an hour.

(EMILIE *exits to the kitchen*)

FELIX. Oh dear, oh dear. (*He starts towards the shop door, decides against going into the shop, settles in the easy chair* R *of the table and carves his block of wood*)

(EMILIE *enters from the kitchen. She carries a tray with a bowl of oranges, a glass jug with a lace and bead cover, and an orange squeezer*)

EMILIE (*crossing to* L *of the table*) I thought I heard the bell, dear. (*She puts the tray on the table*)

(*The mouth-organ music stops*)

FELIX. No.
EMILIE (*moving to the shop door*) I was sure someone had come into the shop. (*She pushes open the door and glances into the shop*)
FELIX. Not a soul.

(EMILIE *moves to the sideboard, gets a knife from the drawer, crosses to* L *of the table and during the ensuing speeches cuts the oranges in half and squeezes the juice into the jug*)

Well, at Christmas time one hears bells. There are bells in the air. Church bells. Sleigh bells. One remembers one's childhood in France. (*He rises, mops his face and crosses to the barometer down* R) Father Christmas. The snow. The angels. The Three Wise Men. Very hot for Christmas Eve, of course. (*He looks at the thermometer*) One hundred and five in the shade.
EMILIE. Then why do you wear that frock coat?
FELIX (*moving behind the easy chair*) My dear, I have a position to maintain, as a business man, as manager of a flourishing establishment in . . .
EMILIE. In a colony of convicts. Felix. You don't think that bell means another thief's been here?
FELIX. Why are you so suspicious? (*He sits* R *of the table*) You're always suspicious.
EMILIE. You ask me that? Living in the shade of a prison full

of desperate thieves, who go out to work, here, there and everywhere free as air.

(*Hammering is heard from the roof*)

Three of them up there at this moment, repairing our roof.
FELIX. My dear, they're perfectly honest.
EMILIE. Honest?
FELIX. They're not thieves. They're murderers.
EMILIE (*moving up stage to stare up the ladder*) They are? Those three—on *our* roof?
FELIX. Most of them are, you know.

(*The mouth-organ is heard playing softly*)

At least, so I've been told. Oh, but they're excellent carpenters.
EMILIE (*moving to L of the table*) Felix, did that boy ever pay you for that mouth-organ?
FELIX. What mouth-organ?
EMILIE. Felix!
FELIX. No. But he does play it so beautifully.
EMILIE. He's out there now. Go and tell him he either pays, or you take back the mouth-organ.
FELIX. Emilie, please! I'll handle this affair.
EMILIE. How?
FELIX. It's a question of book-keeping.
EMILIE. Book-keeping! Felix, you spend hours muddling at your books. If only you insisted on cash we'd be far better off.
FELIX. In any business concern, one must take account of local conditions. What else can one do?
EMILIE. One can ask them to pay their bills. Do you know how much we are owed, Felix?
FELIX. Not offhand. (*He flicks the pages of the ledgers on the table beside him*) But it's quite a nice substantial amount.

(*The mouth-organ music stops*)

EMILIE. Madame Parole must owe us hundreds of francs. She hasn't paid her bills for months.
FELIX. I asked her about it the other day.
EMILIE. And what did she say?
FELIX. She promised to settle up the next time she came in.
EMILIE. Well, she'll be in tonight to do her Christmas shopping. Now don't you let her have a single thing unless she pays. Be firm, Felix.
FELIX. Yes, I will.
EMILIE. She's a greedy, grasping woman who wants us out of here so that her dear Ernest can take over the shop

(The shop bell is heard)

There's the bell.

MME PAROLE *(off; calling)* Emilie, Emilie!

EMILIE. There she is now.

FELIX. Oh, I'll go and see . . . *(He rises and moves towards the shop door)*

(MADAME PAROLE enters from the shop. She carries her handbag and a string bag with a pineapple in it)

MME PAROLE *(crossing to Emilie)* Merry Christmas. *(She kisses Emilie)*

EMILIE. Merry Christmas, Madame Parole.

MME PAROLE *(to Felix)* Merry Christmas.

FELIX *(with a little bow)* Merry Christmas, Madame Parole.

MME PAROLE. I just dropped in for a bottle of Chartreuse—for my husband, you know.

FELIX. Oh, certainly. I'll get you one. *(He crosses to the crates up L)*

MME PAROLE. It's my yearly Christmas surprise for poor Ernest. He always gives me a box of biscuits. Ernest eats the biscuits, of course, and I drink the Chartreuse. *(She laughs)*

(A burst of hammering is heard)

FELIX *(looking in the crates)* Now, let me see . . . *(He searches for the bottle)*

MME PAROLE *(hearing the hammering)* What's that? *(She moves to the verandah steps)* Oh, you still have your workmen. I must say I find convicts convenient. *(She crosses to the sideboard, looks for dust as she passes, then crosses below the table to R of Emilie)* So cheap and so willing. I wouldn't have any other servants. No natives for me. No, thank you very much. Give me convicts every time. Take our man Louis, for example. A treasure, a perfect treasure. Immaculate and what a cook! He may be a little peculiar—shall we say effeminate. But, my dear, he doesn't bother me and he adores Ernest.

FELIX *(still searching)* I don't understand it . . .

(The sound of sawing is heard from the roof)

I had a bottle of Chartreuse here somewhere. *(He moves above the table, then goes to the crates in the corner up R)*

MME PAROLE *(moving above the table)* Oh, it's always the same . . . By the way, Ernest gave me your mail, two ships came in this morning. *(She takes some unopened letters from her bag, examines them, then holds them out to Emilie)*

EMILIE. Thank you. *(She moves to L of Mme Parole and takes the *letters*) While we're waiting—Felix was going over the accounts, weren't you, Felix?

FELIX. Oh, was I? Oh, yes!

EMILIE. And he thought if you could possibly . . .

MME PAROLE. Hmmmmm?

EMILIE. Well, it's quite a large bill . . .

MME PAROLE. But of course, you know how scatterbrained I am.

EMILIE. That's why I took the liberty of reminding you.

(FELIX *takes a bottle of cognac from a crate up* R)

MME PAROLE. Of course, of course.

FELIX (*moving with the bottle to* R *of Mme Parole*) I'm terribly sorry, we seem to have run out of Chartreuse.

MME PAROLE (*grabbing the bottle*) Well, what have you got there? Cognac? Cognac will do, thank you. Now then, tell me, how much do I owe you? (*She feels in her handbag*)

(FELIX *sits hurriedly in his chair* R *of the table and reaches for the ledger*)

Where's my purse? Oh, what a scatterbrain I am. I've forgotten it. Never mind, it can't be helped. Put it on the account, will you?

EMILIE. Well, how soon do you think you'll be able to pay . . .?

MME PAROLE. By the way, how's the shop going? Better? Ernest says you're too trusting, too careless—people take advantage, people are such beasts. (*She puts the bottle in the string bag*) Well, I really must have a look at my bill one of these days. (*She moves to the shop door*) Merry Christmas to you, good-bye, Merry Christmas.

(MME PAROLE *exits to the shop. A moment after, the shop bell rings*)

FELIX. I must enter that sale in my books.

EMILIE. Which sale? Credit right and left. Nobody pays, and thieves take the rest. Thank goodness we still have some of our savings left. (*She puts the letters on the table*) By the way, how much is left, Felix? (*She sits* L *of the table*)

FELIX. Hmmmmm?

EMILIE. Of the money we brought from home?

FELIX (*busy with his carving*) Oh, that money. That's invested.

EMILIE. Invested? (*She picks up a bamboo fan from the table and fans herself*)

FELIX. Yes, I forgot to tell you. There was a mining prospector passing through here with a very attractive proposition. A gold mine somewhere in . . . Oh, I forget where. But you wouldn't understand these things. Believe me, I've been practical.

EMILIE. Then all I hope is, that Marie Louise marries some-one completely impractical.

FELIX. Marie Louise will marry for love, just as we did.

EMILIE. Heaven help her!

FELIX (*rising*) Do you regret it very much?

EMILIE. No.

FELIX. There you are, then. (*He crosses to* L *of Emilie*) Oh, I know we've had our little ups and downs. (*He embraces her*) But it's not too bad here. The heat is a little trying, but as a practical business man I think of all the money I save in coal bills. The heat is free. (*He moves down* L)

MARIE LOUISE (*off; calling*) Mamma! Mamma!

(MARIE LOUISE DULAY *runs in by the verandah from* L)

(*She stands above the table*) Mamma, Paul's here. He's on the *Mirabelle*. I knew he'd come for me. I knew it. I didn't dare breathe it, not even to you, but I knew he wouldn't wait a whole year. I knew it. (*She puts her handbag on the table and moves behind Emilie*) Now do you believe me? Now do you think it's wrong to trust? Blindly? Completely? (*She moves to* L *of Emilie*)

EMILIE (*taking her hands*) Now, now. Will you please tell me. Paul's here? Alone?

MARIE LOUISE. No, with Uncle Gaston. They're in quarantine. (*She turns to Felix*) Papa! You've got to get them out immediately.

EMILIE. You've seen them?

MARIE LOUISE. How could I? I told you, they're in quaran-tine. (*She moves above the table and takes a note from her handbag*) Uncle Gaston sent word through M'sieur Parole for you to get them off the ship straight away. (*She crosses to Felix and gives him the note*) Here's his note. M'sieur Parole gave it to me. I shall do Paul's room myself.

(FELIX *reads the note*)

I know exactly how he likes it. He's not fussy, just particular. (*She runs on to the verandah*) I'm going to get some flowers from the garden. Paul loves flowers.

(MARIE LOUISE *exits on the verandah to* L)

EMILIE. My two children. One I gave birth to—and one I married.

FELIX. Oh, yes. This is a terrible shock—you don't know. (*He crosses to* R *of the table*)

EMILIE. What don't I know?

FELIX. Gaston coming here.

EMILIE. Why shouldn't he? Gaston has business interests in lots of places. This shop's a bagatelle to him. He's not coming down here to . . . Or is he? Felix, what don't I know?

FELIX (*sitting* R *of the table*) In some of his letters he threatened

—unless I reorganized drastically . . . But how could I? With local conditions . . . He can afford to lose a little money the first year, give a man a chance to get acclimatized.

EMILIE. Felix, what exactly do you . . .?

FELIX. You'd think a man who swindled me out of a high-class emporium in Cherbourg, legally I admit, a cousin, by marriage I admit, but still a cousin . . . We grew up together as boys. Just listen to this. (*He reads the note*) "I have two days to give you. I want to do a complete stocktaking and check your books. I shall then make the logical decision. Be good enough to get us both off this damn ship at once."

EMILIE. Logical decision? Felix, does that mean he's going to close the shop?

FELIX. I don't know.

EMILIE. Or get someone else?

FELIX. I don't know.

EMILIE (*putting the fan on the table and rising*) Felix, aren't your books up to date? (*She crosses above the table to him*)

FELIX. Not quite.

EMILIE (*picking up one of the ledgers*) Are they in a very bad way, dear? (*A shower of bills falls from the ledger*)

FELIX. Temporarily, only temporarily. I've been meaning to do them.

EMILIE (*replacing the ledger and papers on the table*) Oh well, we can always go home. (*She embraces Felix*)

FELIX. To what? And with what? At my age. Lord help us!

(*Three loud hammers are heard*)

(*Startled*) What's that?

EMILIE (*moving above the table and gathering the jug etc. on to the tray*) That's not the Lord coming to the rescue. Just some of His wayward children, who'll solve all our problems by murdering us in our beds tonight.

FELIX. Oh, I don't expect so. But what am I going to do about this? (*He waves the note*)

EMILIE. Do? Go down and see the Health people and get him off the ship. (*She moves to the hat-stand and collects Felix's hat*)

(FELIX *rises and moves up* R. EMILIE *puts the hat on his head*)

FELIX. I suppose so.

(MARIE LOUISE *enters on the verandah from* L. *She carries a bunch of flowers*)

MARIE LOUISE (*moving to the whatnot up* L) Papa! Haven't you gone yet? Papa! They're waiting. (*She arranges the flowers in a vase on the whatnot*)

FELIX. I'm going. I'm going. (*He moves to the shop door and turns*) Thank goodness, whatever happens, I still have you, Emilie.

EMILIE. You still have me, Felix.

(FELIX *exits to the shop. A moment after, the shop bell rings*)

(*She moves to the table and picks up a letter*) Here's a letter for you, Marie Louise, from Suzanne. (*She replaces the letter and picks up the tray*)

MARIE LOUISE (*busy with the flowers*) Oh, it's always the same silly letter. At school she was always the first with the bad news. (*She moves down* C)

(EMILIE *moves to the kitchen door*)

Guess who's down with the mumps. Guess who's going to be expelled. Guess who's going to have a . . .

EMILIE (*sharply*) Marie Louise!

(EMILIE *exits to the kitchen*)

MARIE LOUISE (*moving above the table*) I wonder if she's written to me about Paul.

(ALFRED, JULES and JOSEPH *descend the ladder on to the verandah. They wear pyjama-like uniforms with the appropriate numbers on the back, straw hats and sandals. Alfred's number is 4707, Jules' number is 6817, and Joseph's number is 3011.* JOSEPH, *like* JULES, *is in his forties. He is an ex-forger and embezzler.* JULES *killed a faithless wife, is fairly well educated and introspective.* ALFRED, *in his twenties, is an ex-playboy who murdered for money. He carries a coconut cage containing Adolphe. Unseen by* MARIE LOUISE *they stand in a line at the top of the verandah steps.* MARIE LOUISE *picks up the letter, opens it, crosses slowly down* L *as she begins to read, stops and faces* R, *so that her reactions to the letter are seen by the three* CONVICTS. *As she smiles, they smile. As she laughs, they laugh silently; as she bends forward, they do. Suddenly, she gasps and falls to the floor in a faint. The* CONVICTS *exchange looks.* JOSEPH *raises his hat and holds it over his chest. He puts it down on the crates up* R, *gets out his glasses, puts them on and signals to the other two, who move to Marie Louise.* JULES *crosses to her head and stands on the rostrum down* L. ALFRED *crosses to the table, puts down the coconut cage, and stands at her feet.* JOSEPH *comes between them and cautiously picks up the letter*)

JOSEPH. I wonder if this letter was poisoned.
JULES. Poisoned?
JOSEPH. I read somewhere poisoned letters were common in the days of the Borgias. The victim picked it up—poof!
JULES. Well, nothing's happened to you.
JOSEPH. No.
JULES. Yet.
JOSEPH. Eh? (*He moves behind the chair* L *of the table and sets it out a little*)

(JULES *and* ALFRED *lift* MARIE LOUISE *and put her on the chair.* ALFRED *stands* R *of her, and* JULES L *of her*)

JULES. Damn funny though, wasn't it?—there she was, reading away, smiling, chuckling and then all of a sudden—out like a light.

JOSEPH (*standing* L *of* Jules; *having glanced quickly through the letter*) Ah! Here's the poison. (*He reads*) "Darling, Paul and I are engaged. Papa and M. Lemare arranged it just before Paul sailed with his darling uncle. Darling Marie Louise, I know how happy you'll be for us.

(ALFRED *kneels* R *of Marie Louise and pats her hand*)

After all, darling, a schoolgirl crush is not love, as we all know. And let's be frank. That's all there was between you and Paul, and honestly I don't mind. Not a bit. But I do want to save Paul embarrassment when he sees you. You know how kind, how very kind he is." Want to hear any more?

JULES. No. (*He crosses to* L, *drinking in all the details of the room*)

JOSEPH (*examining the envelope*) "Suzanne Roche." Incidentally, she says the night she got engaged her complexion cleared up completely. (*He feels the letter*) Judging from the quality of the stationery and—(*he sniffs the letter*) the general tone of the letter— I should say Suzanne Roche is very rich.

ALFRED. She's a bitch!

JOSEPH (*crossing to* L *of Marie Louise*) I said very rich.

ALFRED. That Paul must be mad. To turn this down. (*He stares at Marie Louise*) She's beautiful.

JOSEPH. Enough of that. You're in no position to admire a beautiful girl.

ALFRED. I can look, can't I?

JOSEPH. You go and get me some water instead. (*He points to the kitchen*)

(MARIE LOUISE *slumps over to her left.* JOSEPH *catches her, sits her straight up in the chair, then moves behind her.* JULES *crosses to* L *of Marie Louise*)

ALFRED (*rising*) All right, Uncle. (*He crosses to the kitchen*)

(EMILIE *enters from the kitchen, sees Alfred and backs away, frightened, against the sideboard*)

EMILIE. Oh! (*She sees Marie Louise*) Oh!

(ALFRED *raises his hat to Emilie, and exits to the kitchen*)

JULES. Now don't be afraid, madame.

(EMILIE *crosses below the table to* R *of Marie Louise*)

(*He crosses to* R *of Joseph*) We were on that ladder when it happened.

EMILIE. When what happened? Marie Louise, speak to me.
JOSEPH. She can't.
JULES. She fainted.
JOSEPH. Nerves. (*He moves above Emilie*)
JULES. Shock.
JOSEPH. No wonder. Read this letter.

(MARIE LOUISE *slumps to her left.* JULES *moves quickly to* L *of her and supports her with one hand*)

Here's the viperish bit. (*He hands the letter to Emilie*)

(ALFRED *enters from the kitchen, carrying a glass of water*)

Believe me, madame, we sympathize with you; Uncle Gaston's unexpected and unwelcome arrival. The fickle Paul! And she had such high hopes. (*He takes the glass from Alfred*)

(JULES *turns Marie Louise's face towards Joseph*)

(*He flicks a few drops of water from the glass on to Marie Louise, then takes a sip of the water*) This is no good, it's too warm. (*He puts the glass on the table*)
EMILIE (*staring at Joseph*) Did you hear everything—(*she indicates the roof*) up there?
JOSEPH. Everything, madame.

(MARIE LOUISE *starts to revive*)

EMILIE. Oh!
JULES. She's coming round, madame. Now, when she opens her eyes, it *might* be a good idea if she sees you first.

(*The three* CONVICTS *stand in a line above the table*)

While we know a great deal about her, she doesn't know very much about us, and she might be a little bit frightened.
EMILIE. Darling . . .
MARIE LOUISE (*sitting up*) Where am . . .? What happ——? (*She sees the Convicts and screams*) Oh!

(ALFRED *puts his hat over Joseph's face*)

EMILIE. Now don't be afraid.
MARIE LOUISE (*rising slowly*) I'm not afraid, Mamma. Nothing can frighten me now. (*She moves slowly towards the arch up* L)
EMILIE (*supporting Marie Louise*) Marie Louise, my darling—I know what it means to you . . .
MARIE LOUISE (*breaking from Emilie*) Please leave me alone. I don't want to talk about it. I don't want to talk to anybody. I don't want to see anybody. I just want to die. I just want to die.

(MARIE LOUISE *runs off by the arch up* L)

EMILIE. Marie Louise . . . (*She starts to follow her*)
JULES (*crossing to* L *of Emilie and intercepting her*) I'd leave her

alone. Youngsters often talk about suicide. We who live on know better. Alfred . . .

(ALFRED *crosses and follows Marie Louise off*)

EMILIE. But—where's he going?

JOSEPH (*moving to* R *of Emilie*) No danger. Everything's under control. Alfred's looking after her. He's quick as a cat.

EMILIE (*facing front*) But she's so upset—so shocked. Heaven knows what she might do.

JOSEPH. Alfred's problem.

(ALFRED *enters by the arch up* L)

ALFRED. Nothing to worry about. She's in her room. I made a thorough search. No poison. No weapons. (*He crosses to the table and puts down a pair of scissors and a nail file*) I removed these. Scissors—nail file. No sedatives—no gas stove, of course—and if she jumps, her window is only three feet from the ground.

JOSEPH (*extending his hand*) Well done.

ALFRED (*shaking hands*) A pleasure—a great pleasure. (*He picks up the cage, crosses and puts it on the whatnot up* L, *then moves to the bamboo post* L *and leans on it*)

JULES (*sitting Emilie in the chair* L *of the table*) You see, madame, we disapprove of death. Especially for young and pretty girls. She'll be all right. Time heals all wounds. We're authorities on the subject of time.

(*The shop bell rings*)

EMILIE. Good heavens! A customer. At a time like this. I suppose I'd better see . . . (*She rises*)

JOSEPH (*stopping her*) A customer is always welcome. May I, madame? It'll be such a treat for me.

(JOSEPH *crosses and exits to the shop*)

EMILIE. Is he going to . . .? (*She stands* L *of the table*)

JULES. Serve the customer? Of course, madame. (*He puts his hat on the whatnot up* L *and moves to* L *of Emilie*) There's nothing he likes better. He can sell anything to anyone—and has.

(EMILIE *looks with uncertainty from the shop door to Alfred, then to Jules. There is an awkward pause, as* EMILIE *backs above the table*)

Do we make you nervous, madame?

EMILIE. No—it's just that . . .

JULES. You've never had convicts working for you before?

EMILIE. Never.

JULES. Well, that's our loss, madame. Our loss. (*He moves the chair close to* L *of the table for Emilie to sit*)

(EMILIE *sits* L *of the table.*
ALFRED, *unnoticed by* EMILIE, *exits quietly by the arch up* L. JULES *notes Alfred's exit, and covers him*)

EMILIE. You don't talk like a convict, somehow.

JULES. Well, I wasn't *born* in a cell, you know—(*he moves above the table*) and then again I wasn't sent here for biting my nails.

EMILIE. Somehow you haven't the face of a—a . . .

JULES. A murderer? No. I agree. (*He pushes the chair above the table, under it*) That's exactly what I said when I caught a glimpse of it in the mirror after I'd . . .

EMILIE (*fascinated, despite herself*) After you'd . . .?

JULES. After I'd strangled my wife, madame.

EMILIE. Oh!

JULES. You see, she didn't think I had the face of a murderer either, poor thing. Now, if she'd thought I had the face of a fool, she would have been right. I was a fool, but I didn't realize it until it was too late. There she was stretched out on the carpet, her poor thin little neck all purple, her eyes staring—in astonishment, I'm sure.

EMILIE. My God!

JULES. Exactly what I said, madame. I called out to Him, but He was busy elsewhere.

EMILIE. Was she—a bad woman?

JULES. Oh no.

EMILIE. Did she make life miserable for you?

JULES. No, never. Never in six years of happy marriage. No, it was my fault.

EMILIE. Oh!

JULES. You see, madame, I returned one day from a trip—unexpectedly.

EMILIE. Unexpectedly?

JULES. *She* didn't expect me—*he* didn't expect me.

EMILIE. Well, you did have provocation, at least.

JULES. Crime of passion.

EMILIE. Well—yes.

JULES. I know. That's what the newspapers called it. But it was stupidity, madame. Sheer stupidity. I should have sent her a telegram.

(ALFRED *enters by the arch up* L)

ALFRED. Madame, the patient is weeping. (*He leans against the pole* L)

EMILIE (*rising and moving up* LC) I must go to her.

JULES (*moving up* C) Why not let her weep, madame?

(JOSEPH *enters from the shop before* EMILIE *can move*)

JOSEPH. Madame, have you got any change, please? (*He holds out a coin*) There's twenty-five francs to take out of this.

EMILIE (*crossing to Joseph*) What did you sell?

JOSEPH. The painting—Madonna and Child—artist unknown.

EMILIE. The painting? It's been here as long as we have.

JOSEPH (*handing the coin to her*) Well, it's gone now.
EMILIE (*crossing to the sideboard*) Who bought it?
JOSEPH (*moving to L of Emilie*) The postmaster.
EMILIE. He couldn't have. He's an atheist.
JOSEPH. He wanted a bedspread.
EMILIE. And you sold him the Madonna and Child? Why, that's a miracle.
JOSEPH. No, madame, a bargain.

(EMILIE *puts the coin in the cash-box on the sideboard and takes out some change which she hands to Joseph*)

I asked him one simple question. How do you know this isn't a Rembrandt, eh? (*He moves to the shop door*) Besides, I couldn't find a bedspread.

(JOSEPH *exits to the shop*)

EMILIE (*moving to R of the table*) Are there very many like you in the . . .?
JULES. In the prison? Well, madame, there are all kinds—a world like any other. All kinds.
EMILIE. Are you all so busy? (*She crosses below the table to LC*) Selling paintings and looking after girls who've fainted?
JULES. No, I'm afraid. Pleasant things like that don't often come our way.

(JOSEPH *enters from the shop*)

JOSEPH (*holding out a coin*) Here we are—ten francs extra madame.

(JULES *moves up C*)

EMILIE (*crossing to Joseph*) Extra?
JOSEPH (*handing her the coin*) For the frame. The article I sold, after all, consists of two items—the picture and the frame. The picture is a matter of taste. Worth a fortune or nothing. But the frame—ah! That's real value. An investment.
EMILIE. I'm a little dizzy. (*She crosses to the sideboard and puts the coin in the cash-box*)
JOSEPH (*spying the ledgers on the table*) Oooh! Books. I have a passion for books. (*He sits R of the table*)

(JULES *moves to L of the table*)

Account books. Jules, did I ever tell you about the night I had to cook the books of a company who were supposed to own three factories?

(EMILIE *moves down R and stands with her back to the kitchen*)

JULES. Tell madame . . .
JOSEPH (*turning to Emilie*) They were air factories, madame.

EMILIE. Air?

JOSEPH. Not compressed air. Just air. For invalids, convalescents.

EMILIE. Oh!

JOSEPH. It was a marvellous idea.

EMILIE. I'm afraid I don't understand.

JOSEPH. Perfectly simple. As you know, doctors often prescribe a change of air for their patients. Well, lots of people can't afford the South of France, or Switzerland. So we had factories at these resorts where the air was bottled. Just like you bottle soda water.

EMILIE. Oh!

JOSEPH. We had two kinds of bottle—a large size to change the air of an entire room, and the small handy pocket size. Inhalers.

EMILIE. And people bought these bottles?

JOSEPH. No, madame. We never put them on the market. But lots of people bought the shares.

JULES. Lots. And all went well until the judge ordered a change of air for *him*—and here he is.

JOSEPH. The judge, unfortunately, madame, was one of the shareholders. (*He rises*) Well—shall we run along? (*He moves up* C)

(JULES *moves up* C. EMILIE *moves up* R. ALFRED *seems far away*)

JULES. I suppose so. (*He moves to the ladder, turns and calls*) Alfred!

(ALFRED *moves up* C)

Come on.

(ALFRED *picks up the cage*)

EMILIE (*moving to Alfred*) What have you got in there?

(ALFRED *shows the cage to Emilie*)

(*She backs away*) Oh, a snake! What a horrible creature.

ALFRED. But, madame, that's Adolphe. He's our pal.

EMILIE. Is he poisonous?

JOSEPH (*moving to* L *of Alfred*) Deadly.

JULES (*moving down* L *of Joseph*) We're very fond of Adolphe. Last year when we worked in the jungle, there was a guard . . .

JOSEPH. A very unpleasant man, and unfortunately incorruptible. He wouldn't take a bribe. A combination of honesty and brutality, madame, is 'orrible.

JULES. You see, madame, he used to love to treat us like slaves —while he lolled under the trees, in the shade. Well, one morning—(*he takes the cage from Alfred*) this little fellow dropped down from a branch right on his big fat neck. (*He snaps his fingers*) Adolphe's a real pal. Look at him—look.

(ALFRED, JULES *and* JOSEPH *peer at the snake*)

JOSEPH. He's laughing.
JULES. Well, we'd better be going. (*He returns the cage to Alfred*)
Good-bye, madame.
JOSEPH ⎫
ALFRED ⎬(*together*) Good-bye, madame.
JULES ⎭
ALFRED (*suddenly*) Wait a minute.

(ALFRED *quickly hands the cage to Joseph, crosses and exits by the arch up* L)

JOSEPH. What's the matter?
EMILIE. Where's he going?
JULES. I think you'd better go too, madame. (*He moves down* L *of the table*) Perhaps your daughter needs you now.

(EMILIE *crosses and exits hurriedly by the arch up* L)

Alfred must have heard something. Did you?
JOSEPH (*moving between Jules and the table*) No.
JULES. Neither did I.
JOSEPH. Ah, youth! Keen ears—keen eyes. Of course, Alfred's always been drawn to romance. Me? (*He glances towards the ledgers on the table*) I have always been drawn to finance.

(EMILIE *enters by the arch up* L *and crosses to* L *of Jules*)

EMILIE. I don't understand it. Marie Louise is not in her room —her window's open . . .
JULES. And Alfred?
EMILIE. I didn't see him.
JULES. Hey! Her window opens on to the garden.

(JOSEPH *moves quickly on to the verandah*)

(*He suddenly moves on to the verandah*) The river!
EMILIE (*moving up* C) I must stop her.
JOSEPH. It's all right, madame—(*he looks off* L) she's already been stopped.
EMILIE. By your friend?
JULES (*looking off* L) Of course.
JOSEPH. She's arguing with him.
EMILIE. I must go to her.
JOSEPH (*moving down* C) You're too late, madame.
EMILIE. Too late?
JOSEPH. Alfred won the argument. (*He laughs*) He's convinced her. (*He turns away to* RC)
EMILIE Are you sure?
JOSEPH. I am positive. (*He laughs and crosses to* R *of Emilie*) Alfred has a striking eloquence. Believe me, madame, your daughter is no longer thinking of ending it all. In fact, your daughter is no longer thinking.

EMILIE. What?

JOSEPH. Knockout! (*He moves to* R *of the table, sits and examines the ledgers and papers*)

EMILIE. What?

JULES (*moving down* C) The only thing to do, madame. If she jumped in the river, what would Alfred do? Jump, too. And then —she would struggle. He'd have to knock her out before he could swim back with her. Well, the technique's just as effective ashore. (*He moves above the table*)

JOSEPH. And not so wet.

(ALFRED *enters on the verandah from* L, *carrying a limp* MARIE LOUISE *over his shoulder.* ALFRED'S *hair is mussed and his face scratched*)

ALFRED. All present and correct.

EMILIE (*moving to them and looking at Marie Louise*) Marie Louise!

ALFRED. She's quite all right, madame, I assure you, madame, as a sportsman. Pulse—normal. I pulled my punch, of course.

JULES. Your efficiency is monotonous.

EMILIE (*to Alfred*) Oh! You're bleeding.

ALFRED. A scratch or two.

EMILIE. How could Marie Louise . . .?

ALFRED. She wasn't herself, madame.

EMILIE. Well, I'll put some iodine on it. In this climate the slightest cut becomes infected.

(EMILIE *crosses and exits to the kitchen.* ALFRED *carries Marie Louise towards the arch up* L.

FELIX *enters from the shop, hangs his hat on the hat-stand, then turns and sees Alfred*)

FELIX. Marie Louise! What are you doing with my daughter? Come back here. (*He turns towards the shop door and calls*) Police! Police!

(JULES *moves down* C.

ALFRED *carries* MARIE LOUISE *off by the arch up* L)

(*He crosses to* R *of Jules and kneels to him*) Kill me, but spare them— that's all I ask. (*He rises, moves to the shop door and calls*) Police! Police!

(EMILIE *enters from the kitchen with a small bottle of iodine*)

EMILIE (*moving above the table*) No—no—Felix—not the police.

(FELIX *crosses to* JULES, *who backs to the post*)

FELIX (*following Jules*) Marie Louise, your father's coming to defend you. Courage—courage.

(ALFRED *enters by the arch up* L. JULES *moves up* C)

EMILIE (*crossing above the table to* c) You don't understand, Felix.

FELIX (*moving to* L *of Emilie*) What don't I understand?

EMILIE. He *had* to hit her.

FELIX. Hit whom?

EMILIE. Marie Louise.

FELIX. Why?

EMILIE. She scratched him. (*She crosses to Alfred and dabs his scratch*)

FELIX. Are you mad? (*He moves to* R *of Emilie*) Defending this —this—brute. Nursing him like a Florence Nightingale. (*He turns and sees Joseph with his ledgers and crosses to* L *of the table*) What are you doing with my account books?

JOSEPH. If you'll forgive me for saying so, I find unspeakable confusion. There's a place for everything, and everything has its place.

FELIX. What? What the devil do you mean? How dare you?

EMILIE (*moving to* L *of Felix and taking his arm*) Please, Felix. (*She leads him* L)

FELIX. But I don't understand what's going on.

(ALFRED *moves up* c)

EMILIE (*leading Felix towards the arch up* L; *to the others*) Please don't go before my husband comes back. He'll want to thank you.

FELIX. Thank them?

EMILIE (*pushing Felix ahead of her*) You don't know what we've been through. Now come along. I wonder if a hot compress . . .

(FELIX *exits by the arch up* L)

JOSEPH. Cold, madame. As cold as the climate will permit.

EMILIE. Thank you.

JOSEPH. Don't mention it.

(EMILIE *exits by the arch up* L)

ALFRED (*dreamily*) You know . . .

JULES. What?

ALFRED. That girl's light as a feather.

JULES. Now come on, forget her.

ALFRED. Why?

JULES. Because the curfew's going to sound any minute, and we've all three of us got to go back to school. (*He moves to* L *of the table and sits*)

JOSEPH. He's right, you know, Alfred. Of course, Jules, I've got no passions. None at all. Except . . .

(*The shop bell rings*)

A customer! (*He rises but hesitates*) Shall I?

JULES. Oh, go on, enjoy yourself.
JOSEPH. Just this once. Eh?
JULES. Why not?

(JOSEPH *picks up the fan from the table and exits cheekily to the shop*)

ALFRED (*moving above the table*) He really gets a kick out of it, doesn't he? (*He sits on the chair above the table*)
JULES. It's the sort of life he was used to. Anyway, you're getting a kick out of it too, aren't you? You seem to be enjoying yourself.
ALFRED. I'd almost forgotten what a home was like.
JULES. Had you? I never have. Not for a single day.
ALFRED. I wonder if it's wise?
JULES. Wise?
ALFRED. Yes, this freedom. When you've been here for a couple of hours, you begin to think of all the nice things you could be doing if only . . . Don't you think we shall regret it?
JULES. No, I shan't. It's good to see a tablecloth again, isn't it? Pictures, nice chairs—look, her knitting . . .

(EMILIE *and* FELIX *enter by the arch up* L. JULES *and* ALFRED *rise*)

EMILIE. My husband has something he wishes to say to you. (*She pulls Felix on and passes him across the front of her to* C)

(EMILIE *gives a warning glance at Felix then exits by the arch up* L)

FELIX (*moving down* LC) My wife's just told me . . . I apologize for the misunderstanding—for my outburst. (*He looks around*) Where's that other fellow?

(JOSEPH *enters from the shop, carrying a white linen jacket on a hanger*)

JOSEPH (*moving to* R *of the table*) The customer wants a larger size. This is a twelve. He wants a fourteen.

(JULES *and* ALFRED *move up* C)

FELIX (*crossing to* L *of Joseph*) I don't believe there is a fourteen.
JOSEPH. There isn't. That's why I told him I'd get one from stock.
FELIX. There's no clothing stock in here.
JOSEPH. I know that. But, I don't sell a piece of goods. I sell an idea. I'll just take this one straight back to him.

(JOSEPH *exits to the shop*)

FELIX. But—he's out of his mind. (*He moves towards the shop door*) The man'll know it won't fit. He can see—feel it . . .
JULES (*moving a step or two down* C) He won't see or feel anything, m'sieu. He won't get a chance to.

FELIX (*turning to Jules*) But it's not fair—it's not ethical. Of course, I suppose you fellows aren't concerned with ethics, naturally—I mean—I don't want to hurt your feelings.

JULES. Not at all, m'sieu. I'm afraid some of us are downright crooked. You see, m'sieu, our world's just like yours. There are all kinds. The only difference is we were caught.

FELIX. Oh yes. My wife told me, and I wanted to thank you. I'd like to repay you.

JULES. That's not necessary, m'sieu.

ALFRED (*bowing*) Wouldn't dream of it. It was a labour of love.

(JULES *looks at Alfred*)

FELIX. Well, my wife thought . . . I'm not sure it's a practical idea. (*He pauses*) In fact, I'm sure it's not—in fact I know it's impossible—but she thought if you would care to spend the evening here—seeing that it's Christmas Eve and all that . . .

JULES. That's very kind of her, m'sieu.

ALFRED. Most kind.

JULES. Very kind.

(JOSEPH *enters from the shop and moves to the sideboard*)

JOSEPH. Sold! (*He drops some coins into the cash-box*) It fits him like a glove. As long as he doesn't button it. Oh, yes, I sold him some cleaning stuff for the spots.

FELIX (*moving to L of Joseph*) Spots? The coat was spotted?

JOSEPH. I made the spots myself. With a little grease. The spots explain the bargain.

FELIX. Bargain?

JOSEPH. At the ordinary price of twenty-seven francs, he wouldn't look at that jacket; but at the reduced price of twenty-seven francs, he snapped it up.

JULES. Joseph, this gentleman has invited us to spend Christmas Eve here.

(ALFRED *moves down L*)

FELIX. Well, my wife thought . . .

JOSEPH. Oh, but what an enchanting prospect. (*He moves to Felix and kisses him French fashion on both cheeks*)

FELIX. Of course, I realize you can't . . . (*He moves above the table*)

JULES. Oh, but we can.

ALFRED. We accept.

JOSEPH. With thanks.

FELIX. But won't the authorities object? They'll miss you at roll-call.

ALFRED. They'll forgive us.

JOSEPH. Oh yes, they're charming.

FELIX. Oh, are they?
CONVICTS (*together*) Mmmmm!
FELIX. But I must warn you—I haven't any spare beds.
JOSEPH. Beds?

(*The* CONVICTS *laugh*)

But, m'sieu, we sleep anywhere.
JULES. You don't know what an armchair means to us.
JOSEPH. Even an armchair.
FELIX. And I must also warn you, my wife hasn't prepared anything special. You know how expensive chicken is.
CONVICTS (*ad lib.*) Oh yes, m'sieu. Don't worry, etc. etc.
JOSEPH. Christmas without a bird.

(*The shop bell rings*)

Another customer. Business is brisk tonight. (*He moves towards the shop door*)
FELIX (*intercepting Joseph*) If you don't mind . . .
JOSEPH. What, m'sieu?
FELIX. Allow me.
JOSEPH (*opening the shop door, standing aside and bowing*) By all means.

(FELIX *glares at Joseph and exits to the shop*)

(*After a look of disappointment*) I'll prompt him from under the counter.

(JOSEPH *exits to the shop.* ALFRED *crosses to the shop door, peers through, then moves above the table to* C. JULES *collects his hat from the crates up* L *and moves to* L *of Alfred*)

ALFRED. Who gets the chicken?
JULES. I'll get it. (*He goes on to the verandah*)
ALFRED. Right. I'll lay the table. I say, pick a plump one. (*He moves to the table*)
JULES. You leave it to me.

(JULES *exits on the verandah to* L. ALFRED *clears the table in the following order. He transfers the books, papers and fan to the chair above the sideboard. He puts the glass, envelope, iodine, file and scissors on the sideboard. He then takes a white tablecloth from the sideboard drawer and spreads it on the table.*
MARIE LOUISE *enters by the arch up* L. *She carries her hat and a little wicker case*)

MARIE LOUISE. Still here?
ALFRED. How many for dinner tonight? Let's see. There's your father, mother, Uncle Gaston, Paul, you . . .
MARIE LOUISE (*putting the case on the chair* L *of the table*) I'm not having dinner. (*She puts on her hat*) I'm leaving tonight.

ALFRED (*moving to the sideboard and taking some cutlery from the drawer*) You're leaving tonight?

MARIE LOUISE (*crossing to L of the table*) Oh, don't worry. I won't try it again.

(ALFRED *drops the cutlery with a clatter on to the table*)

I'm going to the Dominican convent first, then I'll see.

(ALFRED *lays out the cutlery for five places*)

The Mother Superior will understand. My life is finished. At least I can be of service to others. (*She crosses to the shop door*)

ALFRED. You'll want to sit next to Paul, of course.

MARIE LOUISE (*turning and moving to R of the chair above the table*) I told you. I won't be here. How dare you meddle in my affairs?

ALFRED. I asked a civil question. A man travels for weeks on a stinking ship to see you, and you run away from him. I don't understand. You're in love with this fellow. You don't want to live unless you get him. Well, he's here, he wants to see you.

MARIE LOUISE. See me.

ALFRED (*crossing to the sideboard and opening the cupboard*) Why did he come if he doesn't want to see you? (*He kneels and peers into the cupboard*)

MARIE LOUISE. Well, I had a letter . . .

ALFRED. Ah! You believe that Suzanne. (*He rises*) A fellow doesn't travel four thousand miles just to prove he's a liar.

MARIE LOUISE. His uncle made him come.

ALFRED. And where's your trust, where's your faith? (*He moves to R of the table*) How do you know there's a word of truth in what she says? And if there is, and a marriage has been arranged, how do you know he isn't coming here to explain, to make plans to disarrange it. To get round his uncle with your help, your support and your love.

MARIE LOUISE. Oh, no.

ALFRED (*moving to the sideboard*) It's not impossible, is it? (*He takes a pile of napkins from the sideboard drawer*)

MARIE LOUISE. Do you honestly think so?

ALFRED (*tossing the napkins on to the table*) Would he come all this way just to get his face slapped?

MARIE LOUISE. I wouldn't slap his face. He knows that. I don't go around slapping people's faces.

ALFRED (*moving to the sideboard*) I don't know so much about that. (*He takes five glasses from the sideboard cupboard*)

MARIE LOUISE. I'm sorry. I'm terribly sorry about that.

ALFRED (*moving below the table*) Forget it. (*He sets out the glasses*)

MARIE LOUISE (*moving to the chair L of the table*) You really think . . .? (*She picks up the basket and puts it with her handbag on the wicker armchair up L*) Of course there may be something in what you say. He's come to explain—to . . . (*She moves down C*)

ALFRED (*turning to her*) Now shall I lay a place for you?

MARIE LOUISE (*turning to Alfred*) Funny. I believe you because I want to believe you. (*She moves to L of him*) And yet in my heart I know . . .

(*There is a short embarrassed pause as they stand close, then* ALFRED *turns and moves to the sideboard*)

ALFRED. Give him a chance. I'll tell you what—let's toss for it—heads you go, tails you stay. Come on, let's toss a plate. (*He takes a pile of five dinner plates from the cupboard, turns and tosses a plate into the air*)

(MARIE LOUISE *crosses quickly above the table to L of* ALFRED, *who catches the plate*)

MARIE LOUISE. No! No, I'll stay.

ALFRED (*with the plate upheld*) Your mother almost lost a plate.

(JOSEPH *enters from the shop. He carries a peignoir on a hanger, winks at Alfred, then counts up to ten*)

JOSEPH (*calling*) I'm coming, madame. I've found it.

(JOSEPH *exits to the shop.*
   JULES *enters on the verandah from L, concealing a large bulge under his blouse. He crosses, whistling to himself, to the kitchen.* ALFRED *stops him at the kitchen door with an interrogative whistle.* JULES *replies with a whistle, and* ALFRED *comments with a similar whistle.*
   JULES *exits to the kitchen. There is a pause, which is broken by* ALFRED *setting out the plates on the table*)

MARIE LOUISE. Tell me—I know I shouldn't ask . . .

ALFRED. Why was I sent here? That's all right, m'selle. They all want to know that.

MARIE LOUISE. Was it a political crime?

ALFRED. Politics? Women, yes. Horses, yes. But politics—no.

MARIE LOUISE. Were you . . .?

ALFRED. Innocent? Guilty as hell!

MARIE LOUISE. You stole from somebody perhaps?

ALFRED. Well, I'm afraid that was the general idea—yes.

MARIE LOUISE. You were hungry?

ALFRED (*moving to L of Marie Louise*) I'd just had a magnificent dinner at *Maxim's* with a woman, who I thought at the time was the most beautiful woman I had ever seen. We were friends. You see, I had no money. I depended on my stepfather's generosity to keep her. I beg your pardon—to keep her friendship. So I went to see him. (*He crosses above her to the sideboard and picks up the cruet*)

MARIE LOUISE. Naturally.

ALFRED (*moving to R of the table and putting the cruet on it*) Well, I really went to see his safe.

MARIE LOUISE. Oh!

ALFRED (*picking up a table napkin and polishing the glasses*) You see, I knew he had jewels, money and other valuables. Unfortunately, he was a light sleeper. He suddenly appeared in the library. Very imposing figure, my stepfather. Legion of Honour, old soldier, very deep voice.

MARIE LOUISE. Go on!

ALFRED. Well, he roused the servants. Called for the police. I lost my head. I killed him.

MARIE LOUISE. How could you?

ALFRED. With a poker, m'selle. (*He crosses above her to the chair up L, picks up her basket and bag, then moves to L of Marie Louise*) Your gloves. (*He takes her gloves and whips off her hat*) Thank you.

(ALFRED *exits by the arch up* L.

MARIE LOUISE *pauses, bewildered, for a second, then runs off after Alfred. The stage is empty for a moment.*

JOSEPH *enters from the shop. He moves to the sideboard, spits on the coins he is carrying and puts them in the cash-box. He sees a banana in the bowl of fruit on the sideboard, picks it up, peels it and is about to bite it*)

FELIX (*off; calling*) Marie Louise.

(JOSEPH *quickly gulps the banana and moves to the shop door.*

FELIX *enters from the shop and stares bewildered at* JOSEPH'S *contorted features.* JOSEPH *coughs, emitting a large piece of banana, and staggers off into the shop.* FELIX *watches him off, looking puzzled*)

(*He calls*) Marie Louise.

(MARIE LOUISE *enters by the arch up* L *and crosses to* LC)

(*He crosses to* R *of her*) My poor Marie Louise.

MARIE LOUISE. I'm all right now, Papa. Funny . . .

FELIX. What?

MARIE LOUISE. I can hope again.

FELIX. Of course. Of course.

MARIE LOUISE. He gave me hope.

FELIX. Who?

MARIE LOUISE. A murderer!

FELIX. Huh?

(EMILIE *enters by the arch up* L *and crosses to* L *of Marie Louise*)

MARIE LOUISE. Oh, Mamma!

EMILIE. Yes, dear?

MARIE LOUISE. We're going to have a lovely Christmas.

EMILIE. Of course we are.

MARIE LOUISE (*moving to* L *of the table*) We're going to be very festive—very gay. (*She turns the chair* L *of the table into it*) I shall sit next to Paul. His uncle, of course, will sit over there. His uncle will grunt as he always does. Paul will be so tactful, as he always is.

(ALFRED *enters by the arch up* L, *takes in the situation, crosses to the chair below the sideboard and places it below the left end of the table. He then places the chair from above the sideboard below the right end of the table*)

Then we'll drink lots and lots of wine—especially his uncle. And he'll turn mellow gradually—and begin to laugh. We'll sing— and then we'll leave Paul alone with his uncle for a little while. And Paul'll say: "You see, sir? Our love is steel. No-one—no-one can break it."

EMILIE. Yes . . .

FELIX. The only thing is . . .

MARIE LOUISE. What?

(*The sunlight starts to fade with the swiftness of the tropical nightfall*)

FELIX. They won't be here for dinner.

EMILIE. They won't?

(ALFRED, *with a sigh, picks up the two chairs and replaces them above and below the sideboard*)

They've changed their plans?

FELIX. I don't think so.

EMILIE. So much has happened I forgot to ask you if you'd got them out of quarantine.

FELIX. Well, as a matter of fact, I didn't see the Health people. I—I thought it over. It occurred to me—well, I just couldn't face it tonight—and they'll be comfortable on the ship.

(ALFRED *clears two settings and plates from the table and returns the articles to the sideboard*)

EMILIE. Oh! Well—we'll get their rooms ready after dinner in any case. They're sure to be here by morning.

MARIE LOUISE (*to Felix*) And I wanted to see Paul—tonight.

FELIX. You'll see him tomorrow.

(ALFRED, *with a napkin over his arm, stands waiter fashion between the table and the sideboard*)

You can dream about him tonight.

MARIE LOUISE. I've dreamt so long.

EMILIE. Well, with or without Paul, we still must have dinner, and I'd better see to it.

(EMILIE *crosses and exits to the kitchen, meeting* JULES *at the doorway.*
JULES *enters from the kitchen, brushing a cloud of small chicken*

feathers from his hands. Hs crosses and exits on the verandah to L. *The music of the mouth-organ is heard off*)

FELIX. I may be selfish, but I know I'm not sorry to be alone in the bosom of my family—(*he looks at Alfred*) well, practically alone. Oh, we must get the tree out. (*He moves to the crates up* R *and picks up a box*)

MARIE LOUISE (*following Felix*) Oh, yes.

FELIX. Young man——

ALFRED. Yes, sir?

FELIX. —can you open this box?

ALFRED (*crossing up* C) Certainly, sir. (*He takes the box from Felix*) Got a poker?

(MARIE LOUISE *crosses down* LC *and screams*)

Oh! Perhaps a chisel would be better.

(JOSEPH *enters from the shop*)

FELIX. Over there . . .

JOSEPH. Alfred. Hold that still.

ALFRED (*holding the box out*) Right! Here we go.

(JOSEPH *draws a large knife from his belt, crosses to* R *of Alfred, slashes the box open, sheathes the knife and takes the box from* ALFRED, *who takes a very small Christmas tree from it*)

JOSEPH. What have we got here?

ALFRED. There's our tree. (*He hands the tree to Marie Louise*) I say, they got this one young.

JOSEPH. It's hardly weaned.

MARIE LOUISE (*putting the tree on the floor and kneeling* L *of it*) It's beautiful.

ALFRED (*taking a package from the box*) And here are the trimmings. (*He hands the box to Felix, then kneels above the tree and hands the trimmings to Marie Louise*)

FELIX (*putting the box in the corner up* L) I suppose I ought to do something about that mouth-organ—but after all—it's Christmas Eve.

(JOSEPH *draws his knife, brandishes it, and exits threateningly on the verandah to* L)

MARIE LOUISE (*intent on the tree*) It's France. It's home. That lovely pine fragrance we knew as children—in the forest near the sea.

(EMILIE *enters from the kitchen.*

JULES *enters on the verandah from* L. *He carries an orchid and a camellia. The mouth-organ music stops abruptly*)

EMILIE (*moving to* R *of the table*) Felix—Felix.

FELIX. Yes, my dear?

EMILIE. Felix, I found a chicken in the oven. How did it get there?

JULES (*moving above the table*) Praise the Lord, from Whom all blessings flow.

EMILIE. Oh!

JULES. An orchid for madame. (*He leans across the table and hands the orchid to Emilie*)

EMILIE. For me? Thank you.

(JULES *crosses to Alfred, gives him the camellia and indicates it is for Marie Louise*)

ALFRED (*giving the camellia to Marie Louise*) And a camellia for you, m'selle.

MARIE LOUISE. Oh, thank you.

EMILIE. I've never seen a more beautiful orchid, except in the Governor's garden.

JULES. Neither have I.

(JOSEPH *enters on the verandah from* L, *carrying a large decorated Christmas tree*)

JOSEPH (*moving down* LC) Here you are, you can see this one.

FELIX. Where on earth did you get that?

JOSEPH. Sssh! I'll put the little one away in the box to grow up. (*He exchanges the trees, moves up* L, *drops the little tree in its box, then moves to* L *of Felix*) Oh, by the way, m'sieu, the young man has just paid for the mouth-organ.

(JULES *kneels* R *of the tree, and with* ALFRED *and* MARIE LOUISE, *helps to decorate it*)

FELIX. Paid?

EMILIE. How on earth did you . . .?

FELIX. But he has no money.

JOSEPH. I know that. But we bartered. The young man was wearing a handsome gold ring. You get the handsome gold ring. (*He takes a ring from his finger and gives it to Felix*) Sometimes we don't sell. We barter. (*He strokes his cheek with the knife*)

FELIX. But how do I know he didn't steal the ring?

JOSEPH. M'sieu, how can you doubt his word of honour?

FELIX. But after all, receiving stolen property.

JOSEPH. The young man made that ring himself. Out of a gold nugget he found. He's always finding things—nuggets, watches, bicycles, everything.

(JOSEPH *turns, crosses and exits on the verandah to* L)

EMILIE. Felix, open a bottle of wine.

FELIX. Yes, of course. (*He moves to the crates up* L, *takes out a bottle of Beaujolais and a corkscrew*)

ALFRED (*indicating the tree*) Shall we put it on the table?
MARIE LOUISE. Let's.

(ALFRED, JULES *and* MARIE LOUISE *rise*)

JULES. Let me, let me. (*He picks up the tree and crosses to the table*)

(MARIE LOUISE *crosses to the table and clears a space, in which* JULES *places the tree.* ALFRED *moves to Felix and opens the wine for him*)

A real tree, a real Christmas in a real home.
MARIE LOUISE. Careful now.
JULES. I'll treat it very tenderly.
EMILIE. Now I must get back to the kitchen. (*She turns to go*)
JULES. Oh no, madame, tonight we are going to prepare, cook and serve your dinner. Tonight we are your servants. (*He crosses down* L)
EMILIE. Oh, thank you.

(ALFRED *moves and stands slightly above* JULES. FELIX *moves to the table and pours three glasses of wine.* EMILIE *sits* R *of the table and* MARIE LOUISE *sits* L *of it.*

JOSEPH *enters on the verandah from* L *and moves above the table*)

JOSEPH. Oh, doesn't it look beautiful. I've commissioned the young minstrel to play Christmas carols for us.
MARIE LOUISE. Oh, lovely! (*She picks up a glass of wine*)
JOSEPH. M'selle likes that?
MARIE LOUISE. Oh, yes.
JOSEPH. Good. (*He bends over Marie Louise, sniffs her glass, then crosses and stands between Jules and Alfred*) Beaujolais!

(EMILIE *indicates to* FELIX *that he should give some wine to the Convicts.* FELIX *picks up two glasses of wine and hands them to Jules and Joseph.* MARIE LOUISE *rises and takes her glass to Alfred.* FELIX *returns to the table.* MARIE LOUISE *moves to the sideboard, collects three glasses and puts them on the table.* FELIX *fills the glasses*)

FELIX. The compliments of the season to you all.
CONVICTS (*together*) Thank you, m'sieu.
JOSEPH (*stepping forward and draining his glass*) 'Ninety-seven?
FELIX. No.
JOSEPH. No?
FELIX. Oh, no.
JOSEPH. Oh! (*He holds his glass forward to be replenished*)

(FELIX *reluctantly refills the glass*)

(*He drains the glass and savours the taste*) 'Ninety-four?
FELIX. Quite right.
JOSEPH. Oh, pity! (*He steps back into line with Alfred and Jules*)
FELIX (*stepping forward with the bottle*) You see, 'Ninety-four.

JULES. Yes. 'Ninety-four.
JOSEPH. Bottled the same year that I was.

(*The mouth-organ is heard off playing the music of "Three Angels"*)

MARIE LOUISE (*standing up on the chair above the table*) Listen!
ALFRED. What?
MARIE LOUISE. He's playing *Three Angels*.
JULES. So he is. That was my wife's favourite carol.
MARIE LOUISE (*singing*)
          "Three angels came that night—

ALL (*joining in*)
          That Holy Night . . ."

MARIE LOUISE. And look! Look at the tree. (*She indicates three miniature angels on the tree*) We have three angels on the tree, just as in the song. Only my angels are a little shopworn, a little . . .
JOSEPH. A little unlucky, mademoiselle. They were damaged by the long rough journey here. Fallen angels, mademoiselle.
MARIE LOUISE. I don't care. (*She lifts her glass to toast the tree*) I'm going to drink to my three angels.
CONVICTS (*together*) Thank you, mademoiselle.

MARIE LOUISE *turns to the* CONVICTS *who bow, and all drink as*—

the CURTAIN *falls*

ACT II

SCENE—*The same. Later that night.*

When the CURTAIN *rises, the stage is in darkness except for the moonlight in the garden. The lamps are turned very low. The table has been cleared and the large Christmas tree is on the occasional table down* R. JULES *is sleeping in the chair* L *of the table.* ALFRED *is stretched out on the floor below the wicker chair up* L, *with his feet on the chair and his head on the footstool. The coconut cage stands near him.* JOSEPH *is asleep in the armchair* R *of the table, with his back to the table and his feet on the chair below the sideboard, which he has drawn forward. There is a thunderous knocking on the outside door of the shop.* JULES *wakes and rises. The knocking is repeated. He crosses above the table to the sideboard. The knocking is heard for the third time, much louder.*

JULES (*shaking Joseph*) Hey, Jo! Wake up. Someone's trying to get in. (*He turns up the lamp on the sideboard*)
JOSEPH (*waking*) Huh? Probably the Three Wise Men paying us the traditional visit.

(JULES *moves to the lamp up* R *and turns it up. The knocking is heard again, still louder*)

All right, all right, I'm coming.

(JOSEPH *rises, replaces the small chair below the sideboard then exits to the shop*)

JULES. Bit impatient, aren't they? (*He crosses to Alfred*) Alfred! Wake up. (*He moves to the lamp* L *and turns it up*)

(*The knocks on the shop door are repeated, followed by the shop bell and the sound of an angry voice*)

GASTON (*off; angrily*) Are they deaf in there? Where the devil is everybody?

(ALFRED *wakes up, rises and stands with* JULES, *up* L)

JULES. Doesn't sound like the Three Wise Men to me.

(JOSEPH *enters from the shop*)

JOSEPH. It's Father Christmas. (*He crosses and stands in line with Alfred and Jules*)

(GASTON LEMARE *and* PAUL CASSAGON *enter from the shop.* PAUL *carries two suitcases and* GASTON *carries his portfolio. They react to the men in prison uniform*)

GASTON. What the devil . . .? Convicts!

JULES. At your service, m'sieu.

GASTON. It was so damn dark in the shop I didn't see . . . (*He puts his hat and portfolio on the table*)

PAUL. Neither did I, Uncle Gaston. (*He stands the cases on the floor up* R)

JOSEPH. Allow me to introduce myself. I'm three-o-one-one. (*He indicates the number on his back, then points to Jules*) My good friend six-eight-one-seven.

JULES. Enchanted.

JOSEPH (*pointing to Alfred*) And my esteemed colleague four-seven-o-seven.

ALFRED. Delighted.

(FELIX *enters by the arch up* L. *He carries his jacket*)

FELIX (*crossing to* C) I thought I heard the bell . . . (*He stops abruptly*) Gaston!

GASTON. Good evening—or rather, good morning.

FELIX (*crossing to Gaston*) My dear Gaston—(*he flings out his arms*)

(ALFRED *takes the jacket from Felix's arm*)

—welcome—welcome. My dear Paul, welcome—welcome.

PAUL. Thank you, Cousin Felix.

FELIX. I had no idea you'd come tonight——

(GASTON *indicates to* PAUL, *who takes Gaston's portfolio, hat and gloves and puts them on the hat-stand up* R)

—no idea, I assure you.

(ALFRED *moves behind* FELIX, *and helps him on with his jacket*)

Naturally we'd have waited up for you.

(GASTON *sits on the chair above the table.* PAUL *moves and stands* R *of the table.* ALFRED *resumes his place in line with the other Convicts*)

Marie Louise was very anxious to see you, Paul—expected you for Christmas dinner—bitterly disappointed.

GASTON. Was she? And were you?

FELIX. What, Gaston?

GASTON. Bitterly disappointed?

FELIX. Well . . .

GASTON. Did you get my note?

FELIX. Well . . .

GASTON. Don't lie.

FELIX. Gaston, I never lie. I don't know how I manage it, but I never do.

GASTON. I asked you to use your influence with the Health officials. Did you?

FELIX. Well—Christmas Eve and—all that—you know how it is—I thought—you'd be better off on the ship.

GASTON. They said you hadn't been near them. And if I hadn't threatened to have them all sacked, we'd still be on that rubbish bin they call a ship.

PAUL. The heat was stifling.

GASTON. Yes. We had to wait hours for a cab, the driver was drunk—even his horse was drunk. By the luck of the devil we managed to weave our way here in one piece—we are then greeted by your retinue of servants. (*He indicates the Convicts*) I congratulate you on your ménage.

FELIX. Ménage?

GASTON. Don't tell me they're not your servants. What are they? Your friends, who are spending Christmas Eve with you?

FELIX. Well, as a matter of fact, they are—in a way.

JOSEPH (*coming forward*) The guv'nor means a good servant is always a friend. A bad servant is bound to be an enemy. Believe me, I speak from bitter experience.

GASTON. Well, have our bags taken to our rooms.

(ALFRED *picks up the cage and hands it to Jules*)

FELIX. Certainly. (*He indicates the doors* LC *and down* L). Emilie has given you these rooms here. I hope you'll forgive the primitive quality of our hospitality.

(ALFRED *crosses to the bags up* R)

Marie Louise arranged that room for you herself, Paul. I'll take your bags. (*He crosses to the bags up* R)

(ALFRED *forestalls Felix, picks up the bags and crosses down* L)

ALFRED. Allow me, m'sieu.

FELIX. Oh, thank you.

GASTON. Paul, go with him.

(ALFRED *stops down* L *and waits for Paul*)

PAUL. Yes, Uncle. (*He crosses and comes face to face with Joseph and Jules, whom he waves aside*)

(PAUL *exits into the room down* L)

ALFRED (*knocking on the door down* L) Wrong room.

(PAUL *re-enters down* L *and exits into the room* LC)

GASTON (*calling*) And be sure you lock your room when you retire.

PAUL (*off; holding the door open*) Yes, Uncle.

(ALFRED *exits with the cases* LC. PAUL *closes the door*)

GASTON. I'm no more timid than the next man, but these fellows look dangerous. I suppose you always go armed?

FELIX. No.

GASTON. Well, I intend to sleep with a revolver in my hand. (*To* JULES) Bear that in mind.

JULES. Yes, m'sieu.

GASTON (*to Joseph*) You, too.

JOSEPH. Yes, m'sieu. (*He steps forward*) We clean, oil and polish revolvers—part of our daily impeccable service, m'sieu.

GASTON. You won't get your hands on mine. (*To Felix*) Well, Felix, what are you waiting for! The rest of our luggage is in the shop.

FELIX. I'll get it.

JOSEPH. Allow me, m'sieu.

(JOSEPH *crosses and exits to the shop*)

JULES (*crossing to Gaston*) Would the gentleman care for something to eat?

GASTON. You're the cook, I suppose?

JULES. Yes, m'sieu.

FELIX. He's very good. He did a chicken with almonds tonight that was superb.

GASTON. You dined well?

FELIX. Oh, very well.

GASTON. Congratulations! I had a nauseating dinner. Chicken with almonds! Business is suddenly booming, I take it?

JULES. Chickens cost nothing here, m'sieu.

GASTON. Bring me some fruit.

(PAUL *enters* LC. *He carries a suit on a hanger*)

JULES. Very good, m'sieu. (*He turns to Paul*) And you, m'sieu, would you care for something to eat?

PAUL (*hesitating*) I'm famished. What have you got? (*He places the suit on the wicker chair up* L)

JULES. We have some cold chicken, m'sieu.

GASTON. Whatever it is, have it brought to your room.

PAUL. But, Uncle . . .

GASTON. I want to have a little talk with Felix.

PAUL. Yes, Uncle. I wouldn't mind some chicken.

JULES. Very good, m'sieu.

(JULES *exits to the kitchen, taking the cage with him*)

GASTON. Good night, Paul.

PAUL. Good night, Uncle.

(ALFRED *enters* LC, *slamming the door behind him*)

(*To Alfred*) You there——

(JOSEPH *enters from the shop. He carries a suitcase in his right hand.* *He picks up the portolio from the hat-stand with his left hand*)

(*He picks up the suit*) I have a suit for you to press. (*He throws the suit to Alfred*)

(ALFRED *catches the suit, throws it to* JOSEPH, *who drops the case and portfolio, catches the suit and throws it back on to the wicker chair.* PAUL, *furious, exits down* L)

ALFRED (*knocking on the door down* L)   Wrong room.

(PAUL *re-enters down* L *and exits* LC. ALFRED *follows him off.* JOSEPH, *laughing, picks up the case and portfolio, and stands* L *of Gaston*)

GASTON. You there!
JOSEPH. Yes, m'sieu?
GASTON. Get out!
JOSEPH. How can I resist such a charming invitation?

(JOSEPH *drops the bag to the floor and slams the portfolio on to the table in front of Gaston, then exits to the shop, slamming the door behind him*)

GASTON (*staring after him*)   Assassins!
FELIX (*moving* L *of the table*)   They're really not bad fellows. For criminals, I mean.
GASTON. Now let's get this matter straightened out at once. I have very little time to give you. I have a factory to inspect and some mines——

(ALFRED *enters* LC, *banging the door behind him, crosses to* R *and picks up the case*)

—I have only two days here.

(ALFRED *crosses and exits down* L, *slamming the door behind him*)

Now . . .
FELIX. Gaston, you're tired—it's awfully late—hardly the time to talk business.
GASTON. I'm not talking business—yet. I've sent Paul to bed so that you and I can straighten out this nonsense without a lot of silly chatter.

(ALFRED *enters down* L, *slamming the door, then exits* LC, *also slamming the door*)

FELIX. Nonsense?
GASTON. I suppose you know Marie Louise had an affair with Paul before she left . . .
FELIX. Affair? (*He crosses below the table to* R)

GASTON. At least I assume there was an affair. You are fortunate there were no consequences.

FELIX. Gaston . . .

GASTON. At least, I assume there were no consequences. You're not a grandfather, I take it?

FELIX. Do you mean to tell me . . .? Are you implying . . .?

GASTON. Yes, so there the matter rests. Even a fool like you must know I would never tolerate such a ridiculous marriage for Paul. Remember he is at the moment my legal heir. At the moment. So if you're dreaming of a return to France via Marie Louise—wake up. I don't blame you for trying. I don't blame Marie Louise. As a matter of fact I find the matter amusing. Where the devil's my fruit?

(EMILIE and MARIE LOUISE *enter by the arch up* L. *They have dressed hurriedly*)

FELIX (*miserably*) Emilie—Gaston's here.

EMILIE. How are you, Gaston?

GASTON (*rising and crossing to Emilie*) Pleased to see you, Emilie. You too, Marie Louise. (*He kisses their hands*)

MARIE LOUISE (*with a curtsy*) Uncle Gaston.

(EMILIE *moves a little up* C)

GASTON (*to Marie Louise*) You look charming.

MARIE LOUISE. Where's Paul?

GASTON (*moving and sitting on the chair above the table*) Gone to bed.

EMILIE. Oh! Did you have a good trip?

GASTON (*sardonically*) Delightful!

MARIE LOUISE (*crossing to Gaston*) Was Paul seasick? He's such a bad sailor. I remember once he took me sailing, and it wasn't really rough at all, but poor Paul suffered so, we came straight back. He was furious with himself.

GASTON. You stupid little fool.

FELIX. But just a moment—the child merely . . .

EMILIE. There's no need to insult my daughter, Gaston.

GASTON. I have no patience with fools, male or female. Paul's engaged. Damn good family, and a damn good business. You know, Felix, I couldn't buy old Roche out. So I'm marrying him.

(FELIX *turns away in embarrassment*)

MARIE LOUISE. Oh!

EMILIE. If you'll excuse us, Gaston, we're going to bed. Good night.

GASTON. Good night.

EMILIE. Come, Marie Louise.

MARIE LOUISE (*with dignity*) Good night, M. Lemare.

GASTON. Good night, Marie Louise.

(EMILIE *and* MARIE LOUISE *exit by the arch up* L)

FELIX. I really must register my protest against your rudeness
—your—your insults—your—your arrogance. You had no right
to upset Marie Louise—and her mother. Marie Louise is a very
sensitive girl. A good girl.

GASTON. Dear, dear!

FELIX. It's very late. If you'll excuse me, I'm going to bed.
(*He crosses to* LC, *but is stopped by Gaston's voice*)

GASTON (*rising and moving down* R *of the table*) I'm not excusing
you. I'm not at all sleepy. Now that I've disposed of the *affaire*
Marie Louise, let's get down to business.

(ALFRED *enters* LC, *slams the door behind him, crosses to the
kitchen and exits. As he goes, he takes a handful of the bead curtain and
slams it against the saucepans hanging on the backing*)

Well?

FELIX. Hmmmm?

GASTON. How's it going?

FELIX. Oh, the business? Well, I've spent the first year getting
adjusted—acclimatized—(*he moves down* C) getting used to local
conditions, so to speak.

GASTON. And are you acclimatized?

FELIX. I think you'll find that next year will be a great
improvement. A great improvement. I know the difficulties, so
to speak. I know the market . . .

GASTON. You do?

FELIX. Oh, yes.

GASTON. How much business did we do last month?

FELIX. Last month?

GASTON (*impatiently*) November.

FELIX. November?

GASTON. November's always preceded December. Let's have
the figures for November, if you don't mind.

FELIX. I don't remember.

GASTON. Where are the books. Look up the figures, man.

FELIX. I'm not sure what the figures are. I haven't added up
the totals yet.

GASTON. It's the twenty-fourth of December—technically the
twenty-fifth, and you haven't closed your books for November?

(JOSEPH *enters from the shop. He carries a large sheet of cardboard
and a bamboo stick*)

JOSEPH (*as he enters*) Of course we have. (*He stands above the
table*)

(FELIX *turns in surprise*)

GASTON. What do you know about it?

JOSEPH. I'm the bookkeeper, m'sieu.

GASTON. The bookkeeper! Congratulations, Felix! How much did you embezzle last month?

JOSEPH. Really, m'sieu! Our figures were thirty-two thousand eight hundred and fifteen francs and forty-two centimes. An increase over the preceding month of exactly eight thousand five hundred and eighty-one francs and two centimes, m'sieu.

GASTON. An increase?

JOSEPH. Our figures for October were twenty-four thousand three hundred and forty-seven francs and forty-eight centimes (*He stands the chart on the table*) I am preparing a chart—a graph —you'll forgive the crude quality of cardboard and ink. (*To Felix*) Would you mind, m'sieu?

(FELIX *sits* L *of the table and holds one edge of the chart*)

(*To Gaston*) And you, m'sieu. (*He raps on the table to attract Gaston's attention*)

(GASTON *sits* R *of the table and holds the other side of the chart*)

(*He uses the stick as a pointer*) Now, you will observe here that business declines steadily—in the first few months. That was due to new management—conservative clientele suspicious of any-thing new, etcetera, etcetera—then suddenly in August—(*he bangs the cardboard suddenly and knocks it out of their hands*) don't go away —(*he replaces the board*) with the reawakening of confidence— m'sieu's grasp of the affairs, etcetera, etcetera, the line rises, steadily, up, up, up, up—I expect—and I am a cautious observer —a record breaker for December—right up here. I'll need some more cardboard. (*He indicates the line has run off the cardboard, then takes the cardboard and places it with the pointer by the crates up* R)

GASTON. It's fantastic. A convict accountant. Charts, graphs— he knows more about the business than you do.

JOSEPH (*moving above the table*) The guv'nor has more import-ant things on his mind, m'sieu.

GASTON (*laughing*) Did you hear that, Felix? You have more important things on your mind.

(JOSEPH *joins in the laughter. They both stop abruptly*)

JOSEPH. He creates policy—he guides and directs.

GASTON. Really? Tell me, Felix, is it still your policy to extend credit right and left? (*He turns to Joseph*)

FELIX. Well, one has to pander to local conditions.

JOSEPH. And unfortunately, local conditions demand no credit. You've only got to look round here to see a crook. (*He looks round and comes face to face with Gaston*)

GASTON. What about deficiencies?

JOSEPH. Impossible. The governor has an eye like a hawk.

GASTON. Theft—do you lose much by stealing?

JOSEPH. We have our own methods of dealing with that.

FELIX. As a matter of fact, I've had some trouble over some Chartreuse which has been disappearing most mysteriously.

JOSEPH. Oh, I know all about that, m'sieu. The Chartreuse was delivered to the Café de la Poste. I forgot to tell you. These bungling wholesalers!

GASTON. Well, we'll see when we do stocktaking tomorrow.

JOSEPH. Stocktaking tomorrow? But, m'sieu—tomorrow is Christmas Day. A holy day.

GASTON. Good. Then the shop will be closed, and we won't be disturbed.

FELIX. Can't we wait until the day after.

GASTON. The day after I'm devoting to somewhat more substantial matters. I've some mines to inspect. (*He rises*) We'll go over everything tomorrow. I hope, for your sake, everything's in order. Where do I sleep?

FELIX (*rising, crossing down* L *and indicating the door down* L) In here, Gaston.

GASTON (*crossing down* L) Good. I rise at six. We can start at seven—promptly. Good night.

(GASTON *exits down* L)

FELIX. Good night, Gaston. (*He crosses to* L *of Joseph*) Have you gone mad?

JOSEPH. M'sieu?

FELIX. Fake charts—graphs—preposterous statements. I didn't have the sense to stop you—or the courage.

JOSEPH. The situation seemed to call for boldness—and a little exaggeration.

FELIX. It's not enough to pull figures out of the air—concoct stories about the Café de la Poste. I must produce the stock tomorrow—show him my books.

JOSEPH (*moving to the sideboard*) Oh, books!

FELIX. What do you mean, oh books?

JOSEPH (*transferring the ledgers and papers from the sideboard to the table*) We have all night to straighten them out.

FELIX. It'll take more than one night.

JOSEPH. You don't know my system. You know the trouble with most business men is they think mathematics is a science. With me it's an art. (*He sits* R *of the table*)

FELIX (*as it dawns on him*) You mean . . .?

JOSEPH. I mean that cooking your books will be a delightful treat for me.

FELIX. I wouldn't dream of falsifying—any statements.

JOSEPH. Now let me explain—in business, as in life itself, we have reality and the *appearance* of reality. Now you're a painfully honest man. But your books make you look like a crook. All I want to do is to make your books reflect *you*—the real you. I want to paint your portrait.

FELIX. That's all very well, but . . .

JOSEPH. For example, you might have drunk the Chartreuse yourself, or given anything that's missing to some very attractive native girl.

FELIX. I happen to be a devoted husband and father.

JOSEPH. Not in your books. In them you're a scoundrel, a waster and a lecher. I want to restore your character. I want to restore your faith in yourself, and your confidence as a manager. Armed with my books, you'll go forth and make the books come true. It's as simple as that. And now—with your co-operation . . .

(GASTON *enters down* L. *He has removed his jacket and wears a dressing-gown*)

Hold it. (*He quickly rises, picks up the ledgers and moves to the sideboard*)

GASTON. I thought I'd find you still up.

FELIX (*turning; startled*) Can I get you anything, Gaston?

GASTON. Just your books.

FELIX. My books?

GASTON. The accounts.

FELIX. Oh yes—the accounts.

GASTON (*crossing to* L *of the table*) Don't tell me you want to do a little work on them. I'll keep them in my room tonight. I want them just as they are now—in all their pristine purity.

FELIX. Gaston, your suspicions are—are . . . (*He breaks off*)

JOSEPH. I'm sure the gentleman will apologize in the morning, but if it's the books he wants, the books he shall have. (*He crosses below the table to the door down* L) I'll put them in your room.

GASTON. Are they all there?

JOSEPH. The fourth page is loose.

GASTON (*to Felix*) You don't seem to share your accountant's confidence.

FELIX. Well . . .

GASTON (*crossing down* L) Let's hope I can say I'm sorry in the morning. (*To Joseph*) Go on, man.

JOSEPH. After you, m'sieu.

GASTON. Get on, man.

JOSEPH. After you, m'sieu.

GASTON. Will you get on.

(JOSEPH *exits down* L, *slamming the door in Gaston's face.*
GASTON *exits down* L.
JOSEPH *re-enters, crosses to* L *of the table, sits and produces a cigar.* FELIX, *horrified, sits above the table*)

JOSEPH. He's as sharp as a razor, isn't he? (*He puts the cigar in his pocket*) I thought of dumping the books in water—making the

ink run, the figures blur—but he'd have caught on. He's so ruddy
suspicious. Besides, there was no water in there.

FELIX. I'm relieved.

JOSEPH. Relieved?

FELIX. Yes. Because I was tempted. I might have let you cook
the books and I would have lived to regret it.

JOSEPH. Regret it?

FELIX. Oh, I know I'm ridiculous. But I still have honour left.

JOSEPH. There must be something that we could do.

FELIX. I forbid you to do anything.

JOSEPH (*impressively*) Do you realize, tomorrow morning, at
seven, a tornado will roar out of that room . . .

FELIX. I know.

JOSEPH. And you're not afraid?

FELIX. Of course I'm afraid. If I were put upon a wild stallion,
the fear of falling off would not make me a horseman. You see,
I don't know how to ride. I'm an honest man. I don't say that
boastfully. Nor apologetically. I state a fact. I don't know how
to be anything else.

JOSEPH. You're a ruddy marvel!

FELIX. You may laugh at me . . .

JOSEPH. No, I'm not laughing at you.

FELIX. But that's the way I am. (*He rises and moves towards the
arch up* L) I'm going to bed.

(JOSEPH *rises*)

No, please don't get up. Not that I shall get any sleep.

JOSEPH. No?

FELIX. How can I close my eyes tonight? What's to become of
us? And Marie Louise—Paul didn't even ask for her. Good night.

(FELIX *exits by the arch up* L)

JOSEPH. Good night, m'sieu. (*In the pause that follows, he devises
a plan. After a look in the direction of the room that houses Gaston, then
towards Paul's room, he goes to the sideboard, collects a writing pad, pen
and ink, sits above the table, puts on his glasses, and writes*)

(JULES *enters from the kitchen. He carries a plate with a cold
chicken wing.*

ALFRED *follows Jules on. He carries the cage, and stands* R *of
the table*)

What have you got there?

JULES (*stopping* L *of Joseph*) I'm taking the young man his cold
chicken.

JOSEPH. That's a bit of a small portion.

JULES. It's all that's left. Alfred ate the rest just now. He wasn't
hungry—just malicious.

JOSEPH. Well, we can't offend the young man with such measly hospitality. Besides, he shouldn't be thinking of food at a time like this.

ALFRED. That's just what I say.

JOSEPH. I'll have this for the morning. (*He grabs the chicken wing and puts it in his pocket*)

ALFRED. Here he is, under the same roof with a girl who adores him, worships him . . .

JOSEPH. The situation is in hand.

ALFRED. What do you mean?

JOSEPH. We arrange a meeting.

JULES. Eh?

JOSEPH. At once.

JULES. Good idea.

JOSEPH. I didn't have a sample of the young man's handwriting, so I'm printing it. Listen to this. (*He reads his note*) "My darling. My own. Come to me. I wait. I tremble. Oh, my adorable, my beloved. I shall always be your pal."

JULES } (*together*) Your *what*?
ALFRED }

JOSEPH. Oh—(*he re-writes*) "Your *Paul*." Alfred, give this to her.

ALFRED (*taking the note*) Is this wise?

JOSEPH. Don't argue, give it to her. And be as quiet as a cat.

ALFRED. Right.

(ALFRED *crosses and exits by the arch up* L)

JULES. She's not sleeping, I'll guarantee that.

JOSEPH. Jules, get the young man.

(JULES *crosses to the door* LC *and knocks on it.* JOSEPH *rises, replaces the paper, pen and ink on the sideboard, then stands above the table.*
PAUL *enters* LC. *He wears a dressing-gown*)

PAUL. Yes?

JULES. I'm awfully sorry, m'sieu, but there's no cold chicken left.

PAUL. Oh, what a nuisance. (*He crosses below Jules to* C)

JOSEPH. It wouldn't have been cold in any case. The climate, you know. We have to blow on our food to cool it.

PAUL. Well, damn it, haven't you got anything else?

JOSEPH. We have some warm centipede.

PAUL. What?

JULES. A native delicacy, m'sieu.

PAUL. I'd rather go to sleep hungry. (*He turns towards his room*)

JULES (*intercepting Paul*) Sleep? You haven't seen *her* yet.

PAUL. What?

JOSEPH. You don't think *she's* sleeping?

PAUL (*staring from one to the other*) Marie Louise?

JULES. Of course.

JOSEPH. Who else?

JULES. She needs you, my boy. She needs you desperately. She loves you.

JOSEPH. She waits. She trembles. She pants.

PAUL. What the devil?

JULES. Be young, young man. There's so little time.

(ALFRED *enters by the arch, pauses and raps to attract their attention*)

JOSEPH. Oh, what a coincidence, six-eight-one-seven. Here she is.

(JULES *and* JOSEPH *move up* C. PAUL *moves down* C.
MARIE LOUISE *enters by the arch, carrying the note*)

MARIE LOUISE. Paul! (*She crosses to* L *of Paul and embraces him*)

(ALFRED *leans against the pole*)

PAUL. Marie Louise!

MARIE LOUISE. Paul—dear, dear Paul. I couldn't think, couldn't sleep . . .

PAUL. Neither could I, of course.

(JOSEPH *and* JULES *collect* ALFRED *and all three exit by the verandah to* L)

MARIE LOUISE. To think I doubted you for even a moment. Even without your note, I should have known.

PAUL. Note?

MARIE LOUISE. I shall treasure it for ever. I shall press a camellia into it, and when I'm very old—thirty-five—I shall say to my children: "Your father smuggled this note to me on that terrible night when I thought I was lost. When everything stood in our way. His dreadful uncle. A whole year apart—thousands of miles apart . . ."

PAUL. May I—see the note? (*He takes the note and sits* L *of the table*)

MARIE LOUISE. Be careful. Don't crumple it. Even if you hadn't signed it, I'd have known it was yours. Your words—your eloquence—your love—and so beautifully printed. How clever of you to send a convict for me.

PAUL. As a matter of fact, I didn't write this note.

MARIE LOUISE. You didn't? (*She kneels* L *of Paul*)

PAUL. I wish I had.

MARIE LOUISE. I don't understand.

PAUL. Neither do I. I wonder who wrote this? I can't say I'm very amused, but I'm very grateful. If only you knew how I ache for you—hunger for you.

MARIE LOUISE (*rising*) Then marry me—now—here.

PAUL (*rising*) Now? Here?

MARIE LOUISE (*glancing at the door down* L) What does it matter what Uncle Gaston thinks?

PAUL (*moving close to* R *of Marie Louise*) Ssssh!

MARIE LOUISE. What can he do? Disinherit you? What does that matter?

PAUL. My dear Marie Louise, we must be practical . . .

MARIE LOUISE. We're young. We'll get along somehow. I don't mind cooking and scrubbing for you.

PAUL. You're entitled to a decent home—servants—Paris . . .

MARIE LOUISE. I don't care.

PAUL. You've known poverty long enough. So have I. My uncle can be of great help to us. He may be hard, but there are ways of getting round him, I promise you.

MARIE LOUISE. We don't need him.

PAUL. No, but we need his blessing—his money. (*He moves above the table*) It's going to take persistence, patience, tact. One bends with the wind, one compromises—agrees to almost anything—a marriage of convenience—anything—*but*—when the right time comes, and it will come soon enough—one is firm, resolute, determined. He capitulates—we triumph.

MARIE LOUISE (*moving to* L *of him*) How strong you are—how clever. How brilliant!

PAUL. Well, one either has a brain—or one hasn't.

MARIE LOUISE. You make me so proud. When I think that at home, all this time, you've had to fight him alone. Here at least you've got me to help you.

PAUL. Exactly. (*He takes Marie Louise in his arms and kisses her*)

(GASTON *enters down* L. *He carries one of the account books. He sees them, stops and closes the door*)

GASTON. Charming!

(PAUL *and* MARIE LOUISE *separate quickly,* PAUL *almost leaps*)

Well, Paul—since you have so much excess energy, I suggest you expend it on something useful—these accounts. They're a mess. I want a report on them first thing in the morning. Go to your room.

PAUL (*crossing to* L *of the table*) Yes, Uncle.

MARIE LOUISE (*moving between Paul and Gaston*) Paul, don't go.

PAUL. Uncle, I wanted to explain . . .

GASTON. Didn't you hear what I said? Go to your room.

PAUL (*crossing to the door* LC) Yes, Uncle.

GASTON (*moving to Paul*) The accounts. (*He hands the ledger to Paul*)

PAUL. Yes, Uncle.

(PAUL *exits* LC)

GASTON. Well, young woman—apparently I didn't make

myself clear earlier. For the rest of my stay—twenty-four hours precisely—I don't want you to exchange one single word alone with Paul. Is that clear?

MARIE LOUISE. That's what you want—yes. That's clear. What's also clear is you've frightened Paul—made him timid, abject, servile. How could you?

GASTON. You're wasting your time. (*He crosses and sits L of the table*) I'm not going to let Paul make an ass of himself.

(MARIE LOUISE *moves to L of Gaston*)

He owes you nothing.

(JOSEPH, ALFRED *and* JULES *enter on the verandah, unseen by the others, and stand listening.* JOSEPH *is* R, ALFRED C, *and* JULES L)

It takes two to indulge in these little affairs. If your parents had taken proper care of you, it wouldn't have happened. (*He stops and eyes her shrewdly and curiously*) I take it you *have* had an affair?

MARIE LOUISE (*crossing below the table to* R) That's not true. I didn't want our love to be furtive—and cheap.

(GASTON *laughs*)

Paul understands.

GASTON. Be that as it may, I suggest you turn your attentions elsewhere. You can find yourself a young man—or an older man —I suggest an older man——

(*The* CONVICTS *all take a step or two down stage*)

—with a little money in the bank whom you can hoodwink into marriage. (*He rises and moves to L of Marie Louise*) On the other hand, if marriage doesn't interest you, but the comforts of life do, I should say your future was very bright. Very bright indeed. (*He fondles her*) You're young—attractive——

(*The* CONVICTS *move one quick step forward*)

—you have a desirable air of innocence . . .

(MARIE LOUISE *breaks away from Gaston*)

(*He laughs, turns and sees the Convicts*) What the devil do you want?

(*The* CONVICTS *do not move*)

Are you all deaf?

(*The* CONVICTS *all smile and nod. There is a short pause*)

(*He turns to Marie Louise*) Well, I've nothing more to say to you, in any case.

(MARIE LOUISE *turns away and puts her hands to her face.*
GASTON *crosses towards the door down* L. *As he passes them, the*

CONVICTS *all turn and follow him in line.* GASTON *turns at the door, sees them, and exits hurriedly down* L)

MARIE LOUISE (*moving quickly above the table*) There's something I must know—now. I can't sleep until I do.
JOSEPH. Yes?
MARIE LOUISE. I must see Paul—now. Tonight.
JOSEPH (*indicating the door* LC) Go ahead.
MARIE LOUISE. I can't go to his room. (*She backs up* RC). I want you to tell him I'm waiting in the garden. Please, please hurry.

(MARIE LOUISE *exits on the verandah to* L)

JULES (*to Alfred*) Go and get him.
JOSEPH. Wait a minute. I wonder if this is wise?
JULES (*shrugging*) Who knows? She wants him. She shall have him.
JOSEPH (*to Alfred*) Go and get him.

(ALFRED *puts his cage on the whatnot up* L, *then exits* LC)

(*He moves above the table*) I'm not sure she's going to be grateful to us for this.
JULES (*crossing to* L *of the table*) Perhaps she's impatient to know the worst.
JOSEPH. You know, Jules, I'm pretty tolerant, but that young man is a bigger basket than I thought he was.
JULES. Perhaps he's just cautious. Let's be fair. Caution is a virtue I've learned not to despise.

(ALFRED *and* PAUL *enter* LC. PAUL *is in his dressing-gown.* ALFRED *carries Paul's jacket. He pushes* PAUL *forward and stands blocking the door*)

ALFRED. Come on.
PAUL. Where are you taking me?
ALFRED. Go on. (*He pushes* PAUL LC *and throws the jacket on to the wicker chair up* L)
PAUL. What do you want?
JULES (*moving to Paul*) We're concerned with your happiness, my boy. (*He removes Paul's dressing-gown*)
PAUL. What?
JOSEPH. Someone is waiting for you in the garden.
JULES (*picking up the jacket*) Under the bougainvillea. (*He puts the dressing-gown on the chair up* L)

(ALFRED *and* JULES *help* PAUL *into his jacket*)

JOSEPH. Under the what?
JULES. You heard. Come on, hurry.
PAUL. Marie Louise?
JULES. Of course!

PAUL (*looking from one to the other*) I warn you. (*He looks around*) I'm going to call for help.

JOSEPH. Just because you're asked to meet a lovely girl in the garden on a gorgeous tropical night, you're going to call for help. Gentlemen, what has happened to France?

PAUL. I have work to do—the accounts . . .

JULES. The accounts? Can this be our youth?

PAUL. This is sheer insanity. (*He turns towards the door* LC)

(ALFRED *intercepts Paul*)

(*He turns*) What in the devil are you interfering in my life for? This is grotesque.

JULES. You forget it's Christmas.

PAUL. What?

JOSEPH. You're our Christmas present to the young lady.

PAUL (*crossing and sitting* L *of the table*) You're mad. What can I say to her?

JULES (*moving to* L *of Paul*) Whatever she wants to hear—that you love her.

JOSEPH (*leaning across the table*) You *do* love her? Don't you?

PAUL. Of course I love her. I've told her that.

JOSEPH. Tell it to her again.

JULES. Women never get bored with repetition of those three words. They supply their own variations on the theme.

JOSEPH. Exactly. Let her do most of the talking. (*He moves between Paul and the table*) Occasionally you may be called upon to say, "I love you", and occasionally you will say, "Always and for ever". As it's dark, she won't be able to see your face and know you're a bloody liar.

PAUL. I'm not my own master. She doesn't understand that I *can't* marry her.

JULES. Let's live for tonight. Let's leave the future—to the future.

JOSEPH. I suggest you kiss her.

ALFRED. What for?

JOSEPH. What do you mean, "what for"?

JULES. It's customary.

JOSEPH. 'Course it is. I suggest you kiss her frequently—and tenderly.

JULES (*moving close to Paul*) You behave out there as if this were the most important, the most beautiful, the most cherished moment of your life.

PAUL. But Uncle Gaston—is he asleep?

(JULES *and* JOSEPH *take* PAUL *by the arms and lift him to his feet*)

JOSEPH. We'll take care of Uncle Gaston. You think of *her* for once.

(JULES *and* JOSEPH *walk* PAUL *up* C)

We want to give the young lady an hour's happiness—and it seems to me that you're not going to have such a bad time yourself. You ought to be damn grateful.

PAUL (*finally*) Very well, I'll go.

JOSEPH. There's a good boy.

PAUL. And I am grateful, I am truly grateful—but Uncle Gaston?

JOSEPH} (*together*) Never mind about him.
JULES

(JOSEPH *and* JULES *pitch* PAUL *off the verandah to* L)

JOSEPH (*moving to* L *of the table*) Jules, we make progress.

JULES (*moving to* R *of the table*) Well, it's what she wants.

JOSEPH. Funny, I never thought of it.

JULES. What?

JOSEPH. A marriage bureau.

ALFRED. Women!

JULES. Hey! Don't you think they ought to be chaperoned?

JOSEPH. Chaperoned?

JULES. She's a little overwrought. They have only tonight—perhaps their last night—the garden—the moonlight . . .

ALFRED (*running to the verandah*) I'll break every bone in his body.

(ALFRED *exits on the verandah to* L)

JOSEPH (*moving up* C) Hey, that is not the function of a chaperon, Alfred.

(JOSEPH *follows Alfred off.* JULES *crosses to the door down* L *and peeks through the slats.*
EMILIE *enters by the arch up* L)

EMILIE (*amazed*) What are you doing?

JULES (*rising and turning*) Two o'clock, madame, and all's well. Uncle sits with one hand clutching the bedpost as if it were a competitor's throat. With the other he slashes at your husband's books with a pencil.

EMILIE (*moving above the table*) Where's Marie Louise? She's not in her room.

JULES. She's about somewhere.

EMILIE. She's not in the garden with that young man, is she?

JULES. As a matter of fact, she is.

EMILIE. At this hour?

JULES. Don't be afraid, madame. They're being chaperoned.

EMILIE. Chaperoned?

JULES. Properly. My friends are out there.

EMILIE (*moving up* C *and calling*) Marie Louise!

JULES (*moving to* L *of her*) Please, madame, why spoil the happiness she's been dreaming about for so long?

EMILIE (*turning to him*) She's only a child.

JULES. In your eyes, perhaps, but if I were her father I would say, let her solve her own problem. Please go to bed, madame.

EMILIE (*crossing to the arch up* L) I won't sleep.

JULES (*moving to* R *of her*) You must. There's nothing to worry about tonight, believe me. We're here.

EMILIE (*staring at him*) As I listen to you—look at you—I don't know whether I'm awake, or asleep and dreaming. Good night.

JULES. Good night.

(EMILIE *exits by the arch up* L. JULES *moves to the pole* L, *leans against it and gazes out to the verandah.*

ALFRED *enters on the verandah from* L, *crosses and sits* L *of the table.*

JOSEPH *enters on the verandah from* L *and moves* C)

How's it going?

JOSEPH (*crossing to Jules*) Beautifully.

ALFRED (*glancing towards the garden*) He's a cold fish.

JOSEPH. Well, I do admit that at first it didn't sound promising.

JULES. And then?

ALFRED. He sat there—mumbling about his damn uncle.

JULES. And then?

JOSEPH (*crossing to* R *of the table*) Then they were silent. They looked at the stars.

ALFRED. Not a word from him. *Then* he talked—bumbled. He's quoting poetry now. It took him all this time.

JOSEPH (*sitting* R *of the table*) Some men are slow to respond. You must be fair and tolerant.

JULES. Of course. (*He crosses and stands above the table*)

JOSEPH. You know, Jules, I had the feeling that if the boy were free to think for himself, one could hope . . .

ALFRED. Cha!

JULES. Really? Now isn't that interesting.

ALFRED. What do you mean? He's gutless.

JOSEPH. You're not a fair judge. (*To Jules*) Is he?

JULES. He's very prejudiced, I'm afraid.

JOSEPH. I tell you, Jules, I think he'd be quite a nice young man if it wasn't for his uncle. One man the cause of so much unhappiness.

ALFRED. True.

JOSEPH. He's free, and we're in prison. Diabolical, isn't it? There's no justice.

ALFRED. No, there's not.

JULES. Let's bring him to justice. Let's put him on trial. The case of Humanity versus Gaston Lemare. (*He sits above the table*)

I'll be the judge. Wait a moment, I'll put my wig on. (*He adjusts an imaginary wig*) Is it straight?

JOSEPH. Straight as a die, m'lud.

(*The audience are the jury, the "prisoner" is presumed to stand down* L)

(*Loudly*) Silence in court!

JULES. Oh, what a lovely voice you have. Bring in the prisoner. Mr four-seven-o-seven.

ALFRED. Yes, m'lud?

JULES. Will you address the jury on behalf of the Prosecution?

ALFRED. The Prosecution? Certainly, m'lud. (*He rises*)

JULES. Prisoner, stand up.

ALFRED. Do you deny the evidence? Hurry up. I haven't got all day.

JULES. Please, this is a very solemn occasion.

ALFRED. I'm in a hurry. I need another conviction. I am ambitious. I mean to be Home Secretary.

JOSEPH. I object.

JULES. Sustained.

ALFRED. Over-ruled.

JULES. No! No! No! No! I am the judge.

ALFRED. I am in a hurry.

JULES. Oh well, I'm not going to play if you go on like that. Mr three-o-one-one, will you speak on behalf of the Defence?

(ALFRED *resumes his seat*)

JOSEPH (*rising*) Members of the jury—I say to you my client is no criminal. He is a patriot. He has contributed to the greater glory of our beloved country.

JULES. How?

JOSEPH. Who cares?

JULES. A point.

ALFRED. A very good point.

JOSEPH. Members of the jury, I say to you my client is directly responsible for the tremendous increase in the country's birthrate.

JULES (*picking up the fan from the table and using it as an ear-trumpet*) Would you mind speaking up? I can't hear a word you say. Said it was his birthday, did he?

JOSEPH. No. Birthrate.

JULES. Oh—many happy returns of the day.

JOSEPH. Now you consider how he overworks and underpays his many employees. After a fourteen-hour day, do they go to the haunts of sin, the theatres, the concert halls, the cafés?

JULES. Well, do they?

JOSEPH (*quietly*) No.

JULES. Oh, do they?

Joseph (*shouting down the "trumpet"*) No. They totter home to their wives and enjoy the only diversion left open to them.

Jules. Oh, what's that?

Joseph. Tiddleywinks.

Jules. Oh, yes. A lovely game—played it often.

Joseph⎫
Jules ⎭ (*together*) Vive le sport!

Alfred. Viva!

Jules. Prisoner, stand up.

Joseph. He is standing.

Jules. Oh, so he is. Such a short little man. Have you anything to say? No, of course you haven't. The jury finds you guilty as charged.

(Gaston *enters down* l. *As he takes in the scene, the* Convicts *roar with laughter*)

Gaston (*knocking on the door* lc) Paul!

(Gaston *exits* lc. *The* Convicts *rise and move up* c. Alfred *collects the cage from the table up* l *and they stand in a line at the top of the verandah steps,* Jules r, Joseph c, *and* Alfred l.

Gaston *re-enters*)

Where's my nephew?

Jules. Isn't he in his room?

Gaston. He is not. And you know he's not. Where is he?

Joseph. If you really want to know, he's in the garden with the young lady. They make a charming couple.

(Gaston *moves up* c. *The* Convicts *do not move*)

Gaston. Well, get out of my way.

Joseph. They don't wish to be disturbed. This is their moment, is it not?

Jules. Yes.

Gaston. I've had just about enough of your damned impertinence. (*He feels in his pocket and obviously does not find what he is searching for*)

Joseph. Alfred, the gentleman is looking for something.

Alfred (*taking a revolver from his pocket*) This, m'sieu? (*He moves to Gaston*)

Gaston. Give me that.

Alfred. I cleaned it. (*He holds the revolver out in his palm*)

(Gaston *snatches the revolver, backs a step or two and levels it at the Convicts*)

Gaston. Now! Get out of my way.

(Alfred *retreats to his place on the verandah. The* Convicts *slowly raise their hands*)

JOSEPH. It was in a dreadful mess. The barrel was filthy. Naturally we removed the cartridges.

(*The* CONVICTS *slowly lower their hands*)

We had to.

ALFRED. They were damp, anyway.

JULES. It's the climate, m'sieu.

JOSEPH. Frightful.

JULES. Very unhealthy.

JOSEPH. I'd never put this air into a bottle.

GASTON. For the last time, you scum, clear out.

(*The* CONVICTS *advance towards Gaston.* GASTON *backs below the table and stands in front of the chair* L *of it.* JULES *moves down* R, *round the table.* JOSEPH *moves above the chair* L *of the table, and* ALFRED *to* L *of Gaston*)

JULES. You've no need of a revolver anyway.

JOSEPH. We're here. (*He moves close above Gaston and speaks into his ear*) We'll protect you lovingly.

(GASTON, *startled, drops into the chair* L *of the table*)

JULES (*leaning across the table*) We make ideal watchmen.

ALFRED. We never sleep.

JOSEPH. Twenty-four hours' service.

GASTON. I'll have you all arrested in the morning.

(*The* CONVICTS *laugh*)

JOSEPH. I'm afraid you're much too late for that.

ALFRED. We've been arrested permanently.

JULES (*indicating Joseph*) Not him, m'sieu—he's only in for a brief twenty years.

JOSEPH. Sounds long, but taken geologically and historically— a mere flicker of time.

GASTON. Murderers!

ALFRED. Correct.

JOSEPH. Except for me, m'sieu. I, like yourself, was a business man.

GASTON. How dare you? You're a thief!

(*The* CONVICTS *close menacingly on Gaston*)

JOSEPH. I don't think you're very polite, and I don't think I shall stocktake for you tomorrow.

GASTON. Don't worry—you won't.

JOSEPH. Oh, but, m'sieu, I've done stocktaking for a great many people. I have to draw the line somewhere, and do you know, I'm going to draw the line at you.

GASTON (*rising and crossing to the door down* L) I'll settle your hash in the morning. They have ways of punishing scoundrels like you. I'll see to it that you pay for this outrage. I'll report you to the Governor—first thing in the morning.

(GASTON *exits down* L, *slamming the door behind him. There is a pause, then the* CONVICTS *sit slowly at the table,* JOSEPH *above it,* JULES R *of it, and* ALFRED L *of it*)

ALFRED. He's going to see the Governor in the morning.

JULES. Sixty days solitary . . .

ALFRED. Or six months in that hellish jungle.

JOSEPH. I'm not normally pessimistic, but I say again, there's no justice.

ALFRED. No, there's not.

JULES. Sixty days solitary.

JOSEPH. If we're lucky. If only dear uncle would meet with a fatal accident, disappear—vanish. Anything. (*He turns away*)

ALFRED. He's human.

JOSEPH. I doubt it.

ALFRED. I still say he's human. D'you know what I mean?

JULES. Yes, I know what you mean.

(JULES *and* ALFRED *look at Joseph*)

JOSEPH. Now, gentlemen, please. I am not a man of violence. Besides, we might get caught.

JULES. But it was your idea.

JOSEPH. Oh, was it? Well, I've got a better idea.

JULES. What's that?

JOSEPH. You help me to escape.

JULES
ALFRED } (*together*) Yes.

JOSEPH. I go to his home town . . .

JULES. Yes?

JOSEPH. I go to work for him for one year as an accountant.

ALFRED. Yes?

JOSEPH. I fiddle his books—he goes bankrupt.

ALFRED. Yes?

JOSEPH. Then he blows his brains out.

ALFRED. But he would recognize you.

JOSEPH. No, no. I change my name, assume another personality.

ALFRED. How?

JOSEPH. I grow a beard.

JULES (*indicating Joseph's nose*) What about this?

JOSEPH. I grow a moustache.

JULES (*flattening Joseph's nose with his finger*) Wouldn't this be better?

JOSEPH. I don't know—I can't see from here.

JULES (*swinging his arm as though to punch Joseph*) I could do that for you.

ALFRED. Escape, bankruptcy, a year! I'm a man of action.

JULES. Now, just a moment . . .

ALFRED. You're not backing out too?

JULES. No.

ALFRED. Well, let's go. (*He rises*)

JOSEPH. Now wait a minute. Every man's entitled to a fair trial.

JULES. He's already had his.

ALFRED (*resuming his seat*) True.

JOSEPH. So he has. (*He pauses*) How?

JULES. That is the question.

ALFRED. Simple.

JOSEPH. How?

ALFRED. Adolphe! (*He produces the cage and holds it up*)

JOSEPH. Adolphe!

JULES. Of course.

JOSEPH. An inspiration.

ALFRED. Quick——

JULES. —silent——

JOSEPH. —and safe.

ALFRED. An accident.

JULES. Only too common in the tropics.

JOSEPH. An accident is about to be arranged.

ALFRED. Here we go. (*He rises, takes the cage and crosses to the door down* L)

(JOSEPH *rises and follows Alfred*)

JULES. Let justice be done. (*He rises and crosses to* R *of Joseph*)

(*The* CONVICTS *crouch at the door down* L)

ALFRED. Go, Adolphe. (*He puts the cage against the open slats of the door down* L, *then opens the cage*) Right through the crack. Go!

JOSEPH (*after a moment*) Has he gone?

ALFRED (*looking into the cage*) He's gone.

JULES (*with glee*) Can't you see him climbing up the bed? Right up the post. Adolphe sees the hairy hand, palm upward, as if to say: I want mine. All right, says Adolphe, here it is. Keep the change.

JOSEPH. Hey! I never thought of it.

JULES. Thought of what?

JOSEPH. A snake farm.

ALFRED. A what?

JOSEPH. There's a fortune in it. Think of the demand. Think of all the people who want to get rid of their relations.

JULES. Ssh! Hear anything?

ALFRED. Not a sound. Trust Adolphe.

JULES. Well, as the judge, I should note the exact time of execution. (*He rises, and takes an imaginary watch from his pocket*)

ALFRED (*rising*) He's a quiet worker.

(JOSEPH *rises. They all tick away the seconds on their fingers*)

JULES. Six-five-four-three-two-one.

JOSEPH (*crossing to L of the table*) Shall I say a few flattering words in favour of the deceased?

JULES. No. (*He peers through the slats of the door*)

(ALFRED *kneels and peers through the slats of the door*)

JOSEPH. It's usual. I was thinking of something like—He was a —he was a—he *was* a . . . Yes! It is a bit difficult.

ALFRED. I can't tell if he's asleep or dead.

JOSEPH. I've got an infallible test.

ALFRED. What's that?

JOSEPH. Have you got any coins?

ALFRED. Yes.

JOSEPH. Rattle 'em.

(ALFRED *takes some coins from his pocket and rattles them, then peers through the slats of the door*)

ALFRED. He hasn't moved.

JOSEPH. Oooh! That's a good sign. Oh well, we shall know in the morning. (*He moves to the sideboard and turns down the lamp*)

(ALFRED *crosses to the lamp up* R, *turns it down, then goes on to the verandah, puts his legs through the rungs of the ladder and sits on it, staring off* L *into the garden.* JOSEPH *collects the candle, matches, pen, inkwell and paper from the sideboard, sits* R *of the table and puts on his glasses*)

JULES (*leaning against the pole* L; *quietly*) Those who should be asleep are asleep. Those who should be dead are dead. Our young lovers are neither dead nor asleep. Just half-way between, as they should be. (*He stretches up, turns out the lamp on the pole, and crosses to the chair* L *of the table*)

(JOSEPH *strikes a match and lights the candle*)

Now what are you up to?

JOSEPH. I'm writing the last Will and Testament of Gaston Lemare.

JOSEPH *blows out the match and prepares to write as—*

the CURTAIN *falls*

ACT III

SCENE—*The same. Christmas morning.*

When the CURTAIN *rises, the early morning sunshine is pouring into the room.* JOSEPH *is seated above the table, writing.* ALFRED *is still asleep on the ladder.* JULES *is at the sideboard, pouring three mugs of coffee.*

JULES. Coffee up. Haven't you written poor uncle's will yet?
JOSEPH. One more sentence and I'm finished.
JULES. One more sentence and we're all finished.
JOSEPH. Please! It's much too early in the morning.
JULES (*picking up three mugs of coffee and putting them on the table*) Anyway, you're enjoying the job.
JOSEPH. Why not? This is my masterpiece. Here is the note from dear uncle. Here's my rough draft. Compare! Ink, handwriting. Perfection!
JULES (*crossing to Alfred*) Don't ask me. I'm no expert. (*He shakes Alfred*) Alfred, coffee. (*He returns to the sideboard, transfers the bowl of sugar to the table, then sits* R *of it*)

(ALFRED *gets off the ladder, picks up the cage, puts it on the whatnot up* L, *then moves and sits* L *of the table*)

JOSEPH. I challenge the experts. There isn't a court in France that won't honour the deathbed request of our poor uncle. Listen to this. (*He reads*) "My conscience has been bothering me grievously of late. I have a curious premonition of death, somehow. I am writing this shortly after midnight and ask that this constitute an endbit to my will . . ."
JULES. You can't say endbit.
JOSEPH. Why not?
JULES. You call it a codicil.
JOSEPH. A what?
JULES. A codicil.
JOSEPH. What's that?
JULES. An endbit.
JOSEPH. How do you spell it?
JULES. E-N-D-B-I-T.
JOSEPH. No, no. Stop fooling about.
JULES. C-O-D—Cod, I-C-I-L, codicil.
JOSEPH (*making the correction*) Now! (*He reads*) "If anything should happen to me, I implore my nephew Paul, to restore to Felix Dulay, my cousin, the Gallery Modern which I acquired by sharp practice. I could not face the judgement of Providence if this were not done. Paul, you are my heir, and I beg you to

54

help a repentant and tortured sinner by making generous amends to my cousin Felix. Please, Paul, respect my wishes. Be happy, Paul, as I was not. Be honest, Paul, as I was not. Signed—Gaston Lemare."

JULES. Jo, that's wonderful.

ALFRED. Very, very impressive.

JULES. Be happy! Be honest! That's damn good advice to a young man starting out in life—with a fortune.

JOSEPH. That's what I thought.

JULES. And easy to follow—for a young man with a fortune.

JOSEPH. I'm deeply moved by the old sinner's sudden repentance. It just goes to prove . . .

JULES. What?

JOSEPH. There's a little good in the worst of us. After all, he had a conscience.

ALFRED. You gave him one.

JOSEPH. It was nothing really.

JULES. It was a beauty.

JOSEPH. Nothing—nothing at all. (*He takes all the pieces of sugar but one from the bowl and puts them in his cup*)

JULES. Hey! Do you take sugar?

(JOSEPH *takes the last piece of sugar, halves it, and gives it to the others*)

JOSEPH (*laboriously stirring his coffee*) Treacle!

(ALFRED *rises, crosses to the wicker chair up* L *and picks up Paul's jacket*)

JULES. Well, now that you've finished his will, don't you think it would be a good idea to make sure the deceased was dead?

ALFRED (*donning the jacket*) I have the utmost confidence in Adolphe, I'm certain everything went according to plan.

JULES. When we've finished our coffee, we'll have a look.

ALFRED. Hey! How do you like me?

JOSEPH. Splendid!

ALFRED (*picking up the bamboo pointer from the wicker chair and moving down* C) He's got a good tailor. I once had a wonderful tailor. I think I still owe him some money.

JOSEPH. Naturally! You were a gentleman.

ALFRED (*crossing below the table to Jules*) Jules, feel that lining. (*He lifts the bottom of the jacket and strokes the lining*) Isn't that wonderful?

JULES. Stop torturing yourself.

ALFRED (*crossing to* L) There's no harm in pretending I'm human again.

JULES. You're an adolescent.

ALFRED. You sound exactly like my stepfather.

JULES. Oh?

ALFRED. "Grow up", he used to say. You know, I've been thinking—it's all his fault.

JULES. Whose? Your stepfather's?

ALFRED. Yes.

JULES. Why? Because you smacked him over the head with a poker?

ALFRED. No, no, no! If it weren't for that old devil, I wouldn't be just wearing Paul's jacket—I'd be in Paul's shoes.

JULES. I don't understand you, Alfred.

ALFRED (*replacing the pointer on the wicker chair*) Well, you remember the night . . . (*He moves down* L)

JULES. The night?

ALFRED. The night I dined with Colette at *Maxim's*. Afterwards I went to see the old boy. Now supposing he'd been a different kind of old boy.

JULES. You mean—a real father.

ALFRED. Yes. Yes—someone like you.

JULES. Well?

ALFRED. I'd come and see you and I'd say—er . . .

JULES (*rising and crossing to* R *of Alfred*) Well, what would you say?

ALFRED. I'd say, "Good evening".

JULES. And what would I say?

ALFRED. Oh, something like, "Good evening" and "What do you want, you young scoundrel? Hmm? Eh?"

JULES. Oh, would I? Well—"What do you want, you young scoundrel, eh? More money, I suppose?"

ALFRED. How'd you guess, Major?

JULES. A girl, is it, eh?

ALFRED. That's right, Major.

JULES. Sowing a few wild oats, eh? (*He wheezes*)

ALFRED. No, no, no! He didn't have asthma.

JULES. Oh, I'm sorry. Well, how much do you want, you young rogue, eh?

ALFRED. Five thousand, Major.

JULES. Five thousand? Is that all? There you are, you rascal, go and enjoy yourself—you're only young once.

ALFRED. Thank you, Major.

JOSEPH. What the devil do you think you two are playing at?

JULES. Now what happens?

ALFRED. Then I'd find out that Colette was a tart.

JULES. And then.

ALFRED. And then I'd go on a long journey to forget her. I'd try this place—that place—and then I'd end up here. I'd walk into this shop. I'd see *her*. She'd see me. I'd telegraph you—my stepfather, "Have found *the* girl. We want your blessing."

JULES. Bless you, my children. (*He embraces Alfred*) Come home. All is forgiven.

ALFRED. There you are. Now do you see why it was all his fault?

JULES. Of course. (*He moves up* C) The judge should have given you the Legion of Honour, and put the poker in the Louvre as a national monument.

(MARIE LOUISE *enters by the arch up* L. *She is dressed for church and carries her prayer-book and handbag.* ALFRED *moves down* L)

MARIE LOUISE. Good morning.

ALFRED. Good morning, mademoiselle.

JULES. Good morning, mademoiselle.

MARIE LOUISE (*staring at Alfred*) Oh—your jacket. (*She moves to Alfred*) It's Paul's.

ALFRED. Yes, I know.

MARIE LOUISE. Did he give it to you?

ALFRED. No.

MARIE LOUISE. You look very handsome.

ALFRED. I do?

MARIE LOUISE (*moving* LC) Of course, Paul wears clothes with such—distinction. Such elegance.

ALFRED (*glumly*) Yes.

MARIE LOUISE (*moving to Alfred*) But you look very nice. What is your name? You know, I don't even know any of your names.

ALFRED. Alfred.

MARIE LOUISE. You look very nice, Alfred. (*She turns to Jules*) And you are . . .?

JULES. Papa Jules.

(MARIE LOUISE *curtsies then crosses to Joseph*)

MARIE LOUISE. And you?

JOSEPH (*rising*) Eh? Oh, I'm Uncle Joseph.

MARIE LOUISE. You've been very busy.

JOSEPH. Yes, I have, m'selle. I've been up half the night . . . (*He hastily corrects himself*) Oh yes, m'selle, I've been writing my memoirs.

MARIE LOUISE. I'm going to Mass. Will you still be here when I get back?

CONVICTS (*together*) Yes, mademoiselle.

MARIE LOUISE (*crossing to Alfred*) Oh, M'sieu Alfred, I want to thank you.

ALFRED. Thank me?

MARIE LOUISE. Yes—for everything you said yesterday.

(JULES *and* JOSEPH *exchange puzzled looks.* JULES *moves to Joseph*)

About Paul, I mean. You were right, you know. I was a fool to doubt him. Oh, I know he'll never love me as I love him. After all, I'm only a small part of his life. He has so many interests. But I don't mind. I want so little. Even his uncle must know that.

JOSEPH. M'selle. His uncle knows everything now. I think you'll find he's acquired wisdom overnight. In fact, he's a changed man. (*He beams*)

(JULES *furtively nudges Joseph*)

MARIE LOUISE (*puzzled*) He is? How?
JULES (*hastily*) You'll be late for Mass, m'selle.

(ALFRED *crosses quickly to the shop door and holds it open*)

MARIE LOUISE (*moving to the shop door*) Since you're so anxious to get me off to church, I'll go. And I'll say a little prayer to St Anthony for all of you—(*she turns to go, then turns back for a moment*) and for myself.

(MARIE LOUISE *exits to the shop. A moment later the shop bell rings.* ALFRED *moves to the chair* R *of the table and sits*)

JOSEPH. There you are. Done. My masterpiece.
JULES (*moving to* L *of the table and sitting*) Your *magnum opus*.
JOSEPH (*picking up the will and moving to the sideboard*) There's no need to be rude about it. (*He puts the will on the sideboard*) The codicil to Uncle Gaston's will shall be discovered here—and the note where I found it, there. (*He puts the note on the sideboard*)
JULES. Yes, we have a will, but have we a *corpus delicti*?
JOSEPH (*moving and sitting above the table*) I don't know, but I will write you one.
JULES. No, a body.
JOSEPH. Oh, a body?
JULES. Now just suppose Adolphe missed him—or ignored him.
ALFRED. Adolphe wouldn't let his pals down.
JULES. I don't know.
ALFRED. What?
JOSEPH. Let's have a little bet.
ALFRED. Right. I'm a sportsman.
JOSEPH. I'll hold the stakes.
ALFRED. How much?
JULES. Ten centimes our dear uncle's alive and snoring.
ALFRED (*handing a coin to Joseph*). Taken.
JULES. Right. (*He hands a coin to Joseph*)
ALFRED (*rising*) I'll go see . . .
JULES (*stopping him*) Just a minute. I don't trust you. If he's still alive, you might bash his head in just to win the bet. You go, Jo.
JOSEPH. Me? I'm squeamish. Dead bodies offend me.
JULES. Well, somebody's got to go.
JOSEPH. You go.
JULES. Oh, no. I'm the judge. I never look at my victims. I like to sleep nights.

(*The shop bell rings*)

JOSEPH (*rising*) A customer, on Christmas Day?
JULES } (*together*) No!
ALFRED }

(JULES *rises.*
    MME PAROLE *enters from the shop and stands between the side-board and the table.* ALFRED *and* JULES *resume their seats* R *and* L *of the table.* MME PAROLE *carries an opened bottle of cognac and her handbag*)

MME PAROLE. Well, making yourselves at home, aren't you?
JOSEPH. I do beg your pardon, madame, we didn't hear the bell.
MME PAROLE. I want to see M'sieu Gaston Lemare.
JULES } (*together*) What?
ALFRED }
JOSEPH. M'sieu Gaston Lemare?
MME PAROLE. Oh, don't stare at me so stupidly. I know he arrived last night. (*She brushes Joseph aside and crosses above the table towards the arch up* L) I want to tell him a few things about M'sieu Dulay—the swindler.
JOSEPH (*moving quickly to* R *of her*) I am M'sieu Dulay's new assistant. May I assist you?
MME PAROLE (*handing the bottle to Joseph*) Here, taste this cognac.
JOSEPH. Madame wishes me to taste this cognac? The compliments of the season, madame. (*He toasts the others*) Alfred! Jules! (*He takes a mouthful from the bottle and spits it out*)
MME PAROLE. Delicious, isn't it?
JOSEPH. Well, you must remember the thousands of miles this bottle has travelled—the climate. Travel broadens us all, including cognac.
MME PAROLE. Really! How profound.
JOSEPH. I'll admit it has a little taste of—of . . .
MME PAROLE (*exploding*) There's no taste at all. It's plain water.
JOSEPH. Water? Madame, you do exaggerate.
MME PAROLE. So I exaggerate, do I? Read that label.
JOSEPH (*reading the label*) "For window display only."
MME PAROLE. Of all the outrageous things—ruining my Christmas.
JOSEPH. Madame, this is the wrong label. You don't think a company in its right senses would send a sample bottle thousands of miles. For what? This is a beautiful cognac, madame. I speak not only as a merchant, but as a connoisseur.
MME PAROLE. Are you mad? Read that label.
JOSEPH. Do you believe everything you read?

MME PAROLE. Assassin.

JOSEPH. Please, madame, don't be personal, you'll upset my friends.

MME PAROLE. I want to see M. Gaston Lemare.

JOSEPH. You know, somebody should see M. Lemare, and, madame, it may as well be you. (*He indicates the door below* L) Please. This way, madame. Right in *here*. (*He moves below her to the door down* L)

MME PAROLE (*doubtfully*) He's in there? (*She backs away*)

JOSEPH. Don't worry, madame. It's not his bedroom. He's converted it into his office. M. Lemare is famous for converting everything into an office. Including his church pew on Sundays.

(MME PAROLE *crosses to the door down* L *and knocks on it*)

Don't bother to knock. He may not hear you. Go right in, madame.

MME PAROLE. You're sure it's all right?

JOSEPH. Of course. After all, madame, it's very important for you to see M. Lemare. The cognac is just an excuse. You've come because your husband is unhappy in the Customs Service and wants to be a merchant again. He wants to take over this shop. You want to help him get it.

MME PAROLE. Of all the impudent . . .

(MME PAROLE *exits down* L. JOSEPH *moves to the chair above the table, sits and puts the bottle on the table*)

JOSEPH. We'll soon know.

JULES. This is one bet I hope to lose.

(MME PAROLE's *suppressed shriek is heard off.* ALFRED *rises with extended hand to* JOSEPH, *who pays off the bet.* ALFRED *resumes his seat.*

MME PAROLE, *dazed, enters down* L)

MME PAROLE. He's dead.

JOSEPH (*apparently astonished*) What?

JULES. Did you say dead, madame?

MME PAROLE. I'm going to the police——

(JOSEPH *rises and crosses above Mme Parole to* L *of her.* JULES *rises and moves to* R *of Mme Parole, blocking her way*)

—if you scoundrels had anything to do with this, you'll pay for it.

JOSEPH. Madame, if you go to the police, we'll have to tell them . . .

MME PAROLE. Tell them what?

JOSEPH. That we saw you coming out of his bedroom after your little rendezvous.

MME PAROLE. Rendezvous?

JULES. Madame, what were you doing in his bedroom?

MME PAROLE (*indicating Joseph*) He told me to go into that room.

JOSEPH. Oh! A fascinating story. So romantic.

JULES. Yes, but what a shocking *affaire*. Well-known business man expires in ecstasy.

MME PAROLE. But . . .

JOSEPH. A beautiful death.

JULES. Oh, lovely.

JOSEPH. Madame, you have nothing to reproach yourself with. You gave yourself to him to help your husband. Your husband will understand. Yourhusband stayed up all last night on the ships working for you. And you stayed up all night here working for him.

MME PAROLE. How dare you?

JOSEPH. Behind every successful man is a devoted wife. Yes, we have quite a story to tell the police. Shall we come with you?

(JULES *moves to the shop door.* MME PAROLE *backs slowly above the table, closely followed by* JOSEPH)

MME PAROLE. I'm not going to the police. I'm going home.

JOSEPH. Oh, pity. (*He seizes her arm*) By the way—I just remembered. You have a bill. Quite a large bill. It's time you paid.

MME PAROLE. I'll see to it in a day or two. (*She turns to go*)

JOSEPH (*restraining her*) How about a little something on account. (*He eyes her handbag*) I'll bet you have a few hundred francs in there. (*He takes hold of the bag*) Yesterday was pay day for the Customs and you have a model husband. Hands his wages straight over to you.

MME PAROLE. I haven't any money with me.

JOSEPH (*slapping her hand*) Naughty, naughty, naughty.

(MME PAROLE *releases the bag*)

(*He slips the bag off her arm*) I'll bet you have. Shall we have a look together?

MME PAROLE. How dare you?

JOSEPH. What'd you say?

MME PAROLE (*frightened*) Nothing.

(JOSEPH *looks through the contents of the bag*)

I need that money. I've some shopping to do.

JOSEPH. Don't tell me this is the only shop that gives you credit.

MME PAROLE. Certainly not.

JOSEPH. Certainly not. I was right. (*He takes three coins from the bag*) Here we are. Three hundred francs. I congratulate you, madame. I'll credit your account. Alfred, make a note of it.

MME PAROLE. But . . .

JOSEPH (*returning the bag to her*) Your bag, madame, good-bye, good-bye. Oh, don't forget your cognac. (*He picks up the bottle and hands it to her*) Keep it well corked and at room temperature. I recommend you to use a ballroom glass. Warm it with your hands to bring out the bouquet. And sip it. Don't swill.

(MME PAROLE *exits to the shop. The* CONVICTS *laugh.* JOSEPH *hands the coins to* JULES, *who puts them in the cash-box*)

(*He sits above the table*) Hey! We'd better find Adolphe.
JULES. Yes.
ALFRED (*rising*) I'll get him. (*He crosses to the whatnot up* L *and picks up the cage, then moves to the door down* L)
JULES. Now use a towel on Adolphe, Alfred.
JOSEPH. Be careful.
ALFRED. That's all right. I'll handle Adolphe.
JULES. Good luck. (*He crosses and sits* L *of the table*)

(ALFRED *exits down* L)

JOSEPH. You know, Jules, I can't help feeling the world will be a much better place without our dear old uncle.
JULES. Still we face the old, old problem—does the end justify the means?
JOSEPH. Of course it does.
JULES. I wonder.
JOSEPH. My philosophy is simple. If I perpetrate an outrage, it's justifiable. It's moral. It's noble. If someone else does it—it's a ruddy outrage.

(ALFRED *enters down* L)

ALFRED (*crossing to* L *of the table*) I can't find Adolphe!
JOSEPH⎫
JULES ⎭(*together; galvanized*) What?
JOSEPH. Did you look in the bed?
ALFRED. Of course.
JULES (*rising*) We've got to find him.
ALFRED. I looked everywhere. The window is shut tight. He may have crawled back in here.
JOSEPH (*rising quickly*) In here?

(*They all start to look frantically for Adolphe.* ALFRED *moves up* L, *picks up the pointer from the chair, moves down* L, *drops on his knees and pokes under the rostrum.* JULES *crosses to the hat-stand and searches among the crates up* R)

(*He looks around and under the table*) We can't leave him loose in here. He's got no judgement when he bites. Besides, how can he tell the difference between good and evil without us to guide him?
ALFRED. Perhaps he's crawled off somewhere. Maybe he's sick—(*anxiously*) or dying.

JOSEPH (*crawling under the table*) Our dear uncle was highly indigestible, even for a snake.

(JULES *looks on the sideboard.*
PAUL *enters* LC)

PAUL. Where are my . . .?

(ALFRED, *seeing two feet at his eye level, pokes under the trouser legs with the pointer*)

Ooh!

JOSEPH (*straightening up*) We were just looking for a collar stud.

PAUL (*staring down at Alfred*) What the devil are you doing in my jacket?

JOSEPH (*crossing quickly to* R *of Paul*) The valet was just brushing it, sir.

PAUL. Does he have to wear it to brush it?

JOSEPH. It's a local custom he's acquired. (*He crosses below Paul to Alfred*) Alfred, take the gentleman's clothes to his room. And while you're there, I suggest you look for the collar stud.

(ALFRED *rises and exits* LC)

PAUL. What collar stud? Mine?

JOSEPH. No. A native product.

PAUL. I can't wait to get out of this damn country.

(PAUL *exits* LC)

JOSEPH. We can't wait for you to go. (*He moves above the table*) Jules! It's just occurred to me. We should look a bit higher. Adolphe likes heights, trees. If he's strolled out into the garden, we're going to have a devil of a job finding him. (*He climbs on to the table and peers at the hanging lamp*)

(EMILIE *enters by the arch up* L. JULES *stands on the chair above the sideboard and inspects the drape by the shop door*)

Oh! Good morning, madame.

EMILIE (*moving down* C) Looking for something?

JOSEPH. A collar stud.

EMILIE. On the ceiling?

JOSEPH (*getting down from the table and moving up* C) Like other laws, the law of gravity doesn't always work. If you will excuse me—I'll go and look in the garden, madame. You know how collar studs roll.

(JOSEPH *exits on the verandah to* L. EMILIE *follows him a few steps, and watches him off in amazement*)

EMILIE. What a strange man. Is M. Lemare still asleep?

JULES (*nodding*) Dead—to the world. (*He searches around the sideboard*)

(EMILIE *is about to sit in the chair* L *of the table*)

(*He shouts*) No! (*He moves quickly to the chair* L, *picks it up, turns it over, examines it, taps it on the floor, then sure that Adolphe is not on it, he places the chair for Emilie to sit*) Madame?

(EMILIE *sits* L *of the table*)

(*He crosses to the sideboard*) Coffee, madame? (*He kicks the sideboard cupboard doors open, inspects the interior closely, takes out a cup, saucer and spoon, picks up the coffee-pot from the sideboard and crosses to the table*)
EMILIE. Thank you. You'll be leaving us today, won't you?
JULES (*standing above the table*) Yes, madame. All four of us, I hope. (*He pours a cup of coffee for Emilie*)
EMILIE. Four?
JULES. Adolphe, our pet. (*He hands her the coffee*)
EMILIE (*shuddering*) Oh! Thank you. (*She takes the coffee*) It's been interesting—your visit here.
JULES. It's been interesting for us, too.
EMILIE. Thank you. I want you to know—I don't know how to say this——

(JULES *moves down* R *of the table and shakes the edge of the cloth*)

—but I want you to know that I don't blame you for what you did . . . (*She turns and catches Jules shaking the cloth*) That isn't what I meant to say.

(JULES *lifts the cushion of the chair* R *of the table and looks underneath it*)

About your wife, I mean. (*She turns towards Jules and sees him inspecting the cushion*) It may console you a little to know that others, too, have these impulses—wild, almost uncontrollable impulses—I had such an impulse last night, as I was trying to fall off to sleep.
JULES (*for the first time giving her his full attention*) You? You wanted to kill somebody?
EMILIE. Gaston Lemare.
JULES (*laughing*) Oh, excuse me, madame. Him? You wanted to kill him?
EMILIE. Oh, I know you think me ridiculous.
JULES. Not a bit.
EMILIE. It's absurd, of course.
JULES. Of course. Tell me, madame—(*he sits on the chair above the table*) just how did *you* plan to exterminate M. Lemare?
EMILIE. My crime was all in my mind.
JULES (*smiling*) Of course. No, you could never do it, madame

—under any circumstances. Think it? Yes. Perhaps even plan it. But actually do it . . . (*He shakes his head*)

EMILIE. Felix wouldn't even let himself think it—poor Felix.

JULES. Why poor Felix? He's happy. And you're not unhappy, are you?

EMILIE. I suppose not. I know that in a few hours, many dreadful things may happen. We may be shipped back to France, penniless, with no prospects, nothing. Heaven knows what we'll do. But somehow, I find myself echoing Felix: "Things will work out somehow. There's always hope."

JULES. He is right. Hope is everything. Even we have hope. We hope to escape—although we know we'll never do it. We hope for a pardon, although we know we'll never get it.

EMILIE (*rising and moving above the chair L of the table*) You know, sometimes I can't help wondering if I wouldn't have made a better wife for a man who wasn't a child—someone who didn't believe in fairy tales—who depended not on others, but on himself—and a little on me.

JULES. Men like that have no reason to marry.

EMILIE. You did.

JULES. Me? I believed in fairy tales, too—and when I stumbled on reality, I killed. (*He rises*) You know what *I* was thinking when *I* finally fell off to sleep last night?

EMILIE. What?

JULES. I was thinking—if I had married a woman like you— perhaps I wouldn't be here.

EMILIE (*touched and excited*) More coffee.

JULES. No, thank you.

EMILIE (*sitting L of the table*) I'm beginning to wonder what is the matter with me this morning. I'm really feeling—thinking— saying—the most absurd—ridiculous . . .

JULES. Thank you for saying them.

EMILIE. I'm beginning to believe I'm the romantic—not Felix.

JULES. Yes . . .

EMILIE. I'm really not myself.

JULES (*leaning across the table*) Thank you for this Christmas— it'll be a treasured memory. A man in my position doesn't store up many memories—and you—when you get back home to your Brittany—to the kind of home you should have—all this will be an amusing story for a dull dinner party.

EMILIE. I don't see a future of dinner parties, dull or otherwise.

JULES. Remember—hope. Things will work out somehow.

(PAUL, *looking back over his shoulder, enters* LC)

Perhaps *he'll* work them out.

EMILIE. Paul!

(JULES *moves to the sideboard, collects a cup, saucer and spoon and puts them on the table*)

PAUL (*turning and crossing to Emilie*) Good morning, madame. (*He kisses her hand*)

EMILIE. How nice to see you.

PAUL. I'm sorry I missed you last night.

(JULES *pours a cup of coffee*)

EMILIE. That's quite all right.

PAUL. That's a strange valet you have.

EMILIE. Valet?

JULES. Alfred, madame.

PAUL. He's standing on the bed with his dirty feet and staring at the ceiling.

JULES (*picking up the cup of coffee and offering it to Paul*) He's looking for native wild life, m'sieu. He's a great student of nature.

(PAUL *moves above the table and takes the coffee.*
FELIX *enters by the arch up L and crosses to LC*)

FELIX. Good morning, Paul.

(JULES *moves to the sideboard and collects a cup, saucer and spoon*)

PAUL. Good morning, Cousin Felix.

FELIX. Where is Gaston?

EMILIE. He's still asleep.

PAUL. Asleep? (*He puts his cup on the table*) But that's impossible.

EMILIE. Why?

PAUL. He never sleeps as late as this. (*He looks at his watch*) He's always up at six o'clock. He says it's the early bird that gets the worm.

(JULES *rattles the cup and saucer on the sideboard*)

I don't understand it. I'm sure he'd want me to wake him. (*He crosses to the door down L*) He said he had a lot to do today.

FELIX. Well—why not let him sleep?

(JULES *transfers the cup and saucer to the table and fills it with coffee*)

PAUL. Then he'll think *I* overslept. I'd better go in and see.

(PAUL *knocks at the door down L, pauses a moment, then exits*)

JULES (*to Felix*) Coffee, m'sieu?

FELIX. Oh, thank you. (*He moves below the table, picks up his coffee, then crosses to the barometer*)

EMILIE. I do hope nothing's happened.

JULES. Do you?

FELIX. Beautiful day. (*He looks at the thermometer*) Only a hundred and four in the shade.

(ALFRED *enters* LC, *crosses to Jules and shakes his head.* JULES
signals him to wait quietly. There is a short pause.
      PAUL, *looking dazed, enters down* L)

(*He crosses to Paul*) What's the matter?
PAUL. My uncle—is—is—dead.

   (EMILIE *rises*)

ALFRED. Dead as a doornail. But where the hell is Adolphe?
JULES. In the garden. (*He pushes Alfred up* C)

   (ALFRED *exits on the verandah to* L. JULES *busies himself collecting
the cups and putting them on the tray*)

EMILIE. Paul!
FELIX. Dead!
PAUL. His heart—it must have been his heart.
EMILIE. Felix!
PAUL. I don't understand it. His doctors said he would live to
be ninety.
JULES. He can sue his doctors for breach of contract.
FELIX. I'd better . . .

   (FELIX *exits down* L)

EMILIE. I can't believe it.
PAUL. I don't understand it.

   (PAUL *follows Felix off down* L)

EMILIE. I must be dreaming. (*She turns to the table and puts her
cup on it*)
JULES (*moving to the table and picking up Emilie's cup*) You see,
madame, it isn't necessary to kill. Fate always arranges for the
triumph of good over evil.
EMILIE (*stunned*) He's dead!
JULES. Uh-huh! No need for violence—no guilt—no self-
reproach.
EMILIE. I can't help feeling a little—guilt—for even thinking . . .
JULES. In civilized countries, thinking is not a crime. (*He moves
to the sideboard and puts the cup on it*)

   (FELIX *and* PAUL *enter down* L)

EMILIE. I'm so confused I no longer know where I am.
FELIX. It's so . . . It's terrible.
EMILIE. I think I'll go to my room.
JULES. A very good idea, madame.
FELIX. Of course, darling. (*He ushers Emilie up* L)

(EMILIE *exits by the arch up* L. FELIX *moves to* PAUL, *who stands by the door down* L)

I'll get a doctor to take care of the formalities. Paul, will you stay here, my boy? (*He crosses to the hat-stand*)

(JOSEPH *enters on the verandah from* L *and moves to* L *of Felix*)

I'll be back as soon as I can. (*He puts on his hat*)
JOSEPH. I've just heard the news.

(ALFRED *crawls on to the verandah from* L, *crosses on his knees and exits on the verandah to* R)

We've lost a great man.
FELIX. I would never have forgiven myself if I'd deceived him last night.
JOSEPH. You were right. You've proved that virtue is its own reward.
FELIX. Extraordinary. To die so suddenly.

(FELIX *exits to the shop.*
ALFRED *enters on the verandah from* R. JULES *stares at* PAUL, *who becomes aware of it, and crosses to the chair* L *of the table*)

PAUL (*elegantly mopping his brow*) What a thing to happen. I can't believe it. (*He sits* L *of the table*) This is dreadful.

(ALFRED *and* JOSEPH *stand up* RC, *watching Paul*)

JULES (*leaning against the sideboard*) May I offer my sympathy?
PAUL. Thank you.
JULES (*moving above the table*) You're welcome.
JOSEPH (*moving to* L *of Paul*) Your uncle's death must be a great loss to you—I speak emotionally—not financially.

(ALFRED *moves above Paul*)

PAUL. Oh, yes.
JOSEPH. A great loss. (*He signals to Jules*)

(JULES *moves to the sideboard and picks up the will*)

JULES. Oh, there seems to be a letter here for you, m'sieu. (*He crosses to Paul*)
PAUL. For me? Thank you. (*He takes the will and stares at the writing*) From Uncle Gaston.
JOSEPH. How should I know? I hope you did not mind our little joke last night.
PAUL. Little joke.
JOSEPH. The episode in the garden—under the what was it?
JULES. The bougainvillea.
JOSEPH. What my friend said.

PAUL. Oh, not at all. (*He stares at the will*) It was very pleasant
—very . . . (*His voice trails off, and he crumples the will*)

JOSEPH (*snatching the will from Paul*) That's no way to treat a
letter from your uncle—and him still warm.

(PAUL *attempts to rise, but is pushed down by* JULES *and* ALFRED)

PAUL. Let me go.

JOSEPH. All communications from the deceased must be pre-
served. Have you no respect for the law? All communications. No
matter how trivial. (*He straightens the crumpled will and pretends to
study it*) And this doesn't seem trivial at all.

JULES
ALFRED } (*together*) No?

JOSEPH. Not at all. (*He gasps*) Young man, this is very serious.
A dying man's last request—his last gasp. A voice from the grave.

JULES. Really? Well, I never did.

PAUL. I'm—so upset naturally that—I didn't understand it—
I . . .

JOSEPH. But it's perfectly clear. (*He passes the will over Paul's
head to Jules*)

(PAUL *ineffectually grabs at the will*)

(*To Jules*) It's clear to you, isn't it?

JULES (*pretending to read*) "I have a curious premonition of
death, somehow—to restore to Felix Dulay, my cousin—be
happy, Paul, as I was not. Be honest, Paul, as I was not . . ." (*He
returns the will to Joseph*)

JOSEPH (*glaring at Paul*) Honest! Your fiancée's father. Deceiving *him*. Deceiving the dead. M'sieu, you are unethical.

ALFRED. With all that money he's inheriting—he wants more
—the swine.

PAUL. I have every intention of respecting my uncle's wishes.

JOSEPH. Now that we have this—this—this codicil securely in
our possession.

PAUL. I won't contest it, I assure you. (*He rises and crosses to the
door down* L) I repeat: I respect my uncle's wishes. If the document
is genuine.

JOSEPH (*crossing to* R *of Paul*) If? You doubt this document?

ALFRED (*moving to* R *of Joseph*) What about Marie Louise?

PAUL. What about her?

ALFRED. Are you marrying her?

PAUL. I don't see how that concerns you.

(ALFRED *makes a move to attack Paul, but* JOSEPH *prevents him.*
ALFRED *moves up* C)

JOSEPH. We went to considerable trouble last night to smooth
the path of love.

(JULES *crosses to* R *of Joseph.* ALFRED *moves to* R *of Jules*)

PAUL (*after a pause*) In this, as in all other matters, I shall be guided by my uncle's wishes.

JOSEPH. You realize, of course, that you're now free to do as you please.

PAUL. Yes.

JULES. You're rich—your own master.

PAUL. Yes.

JOSEPH. But Suzanne Roche whose complexion cleared up completely. She still attracts you?

PAUL (*after a pause*) Yes.

JOSEPH. Gentlemen, a strange thing has happened. His uncle didn't die after all. He lives on—in *him*.

PAUL (*crossing below the others to R of the table*) I find this conversation distasteful—and impertinent. Once and for all—my relations with Marie Louise are my business, not yours. I'm *not* free to do as I please—(*he leans across the table*) wealth is a responsibility.

JULES (*crossing to L of the table*) Get out! Before I forget myself.

PAUL. What?

ALFRED. I think I'm going to crack his head in. (*He starts towards Paul*)

(JULES *intercepts Alfred and restrains him*)

PAUL. You can't intimidate me. I'll report you.

JULES (*ominously*) Yes! Your uncle wanted to report us.

ALFRED. Yes.

JULES. We don't like being reported.

ALFRED. No.

PAUL. I believe the authorities have ways and means of punishing scoundrels like you. I had intended to call on the Governor with my uncle. Now I'll go alone, and I'll tell him how his convicts behave. (*He crosses above the table to R of Joseph*) As for that—that forgery . . .

JOSEPH. Forgery?

PAUL. Well, suddenly a note appears a moment after uncle's death. Suddenly! Suddenly he's repentant. I'll tell you what I think. I think you concocted this little scheme. And if M. Dulay was a party to this, and I suspect he was, you may tell him I shall demand an official enquiry. Handwriting experts. And you can also tell him I'm going to have his books audited. A man capable of forgery is also capable of embezzlement. (*He moves slowly to the door down L*) Now, with your permission, I'm going to pay my respects.

(PAUL *exits down L. There is a long silence during which* JULES *moves to R of the table,* JOSEPH *above it, and* ALFRED *to L of it. They all slowly sit*)

JULES. Well, come on, let's have another trial.

ALFRED. Yes.

JOSEPH. No. Please, not *two* accidents.

ALFRED. Why not?

JOSEPH. We'd never get away with it. Besides, we've lost our executioner.

ALFRED. I'll do this job myself.

JOSEPH. No.

JULES. No, wait a minute. Don't lose your head.

JOSEPH. Nasty business—the guillotine.

ALFRED. He doesn't deserve to live.

JOSEPH. That is not the issue. The issue is: do we deserve to live. And according to my slightly biased opinion, I should say the answer is yes.

JULES. Well, at least we want to—even in solitary.

ALFRED. Now look, I'm going to do this all by myself, you won't be involved.

JOSEPH. They'd never believe you.

JULES. And even if they did—we don't want to lose you.

JOSEPH. No.

JULES. We belong together—we three.

JOSEPH. Of course we do.

ALFRED. Oh, well, all our work down the drain.

JULES. We tried.

JOSEPH. We failed. We've learned that virtue is not it's own reward.

JULES. And that good does not always triumph over evil.

JOSEPH. For us Christmas is over.

JULES. We pack away the tinsel—store away the tree.

JOSEPH. And complain vaguely of indigestion.

(PAUL *enters quickly down* L. *He is holding his hand*)

PAUL. This is ridiculous. What a ghastly country! Call a doctor, quick.

JULES. What's the matter?

PAUL. I've just been bitten by a snake.

JOSEPH (*laughing*) What did he say?

JULES. He said he'd just been bitten by a snake.

ALFRED. How—where?

PAUL. What does it matter where? A doctor!

JOSEPH (*rising and crossing to Paul*) Was it a little snake?

PAUL. Yes.

JOSEPH. It was! Where was it? On the floor?

PAUL. No.

JOSEPH. On the bed?

PAUL. No.

JOSEPH. On the dresser?

PAUL. No.

JOSEPH. On the ceiling?

PAUL. No.

JOSEPH. Well, where?

PAUL. In his trousers—in the pocket.

JOSEPH. And what, may I ask, were you doing with your hand in your uncle's trousers pocket?

JULES. He was stocktaking.

(*The* CONVICTS *laugh.* JOSEPH *assumes a serious manner and moves above the table.* PAUL *leans against the pole* L)

JOSEPH. Alfred, this is no laughing matter. This young man has shown remarkable industry and thrift. He has overlooked nothing. (*He sits above the table*)

PAUL. I want a doctor.

JOSEPH. Why waste your money?

PAUL. I don't feel very well.

JOSEPH. It's going to be a bit awkward, him not feeling very well in here.

ALFRED. Of course. Marie Louise coming back from church.

JULES. Think of the shock. We've got to get rid of him.

PAUL. What are you talking about? I want a doctor, I tell you.

JOSEPH. I've got it. The garden. Let him not feel very well in the garden.

JULES. Yes, we'll take him to the bench.

JOSEPH. Yes, the same bench as last night.

(JULES *and* JOSEPH *rise, cross to Paul and each take an arm*)

JULES. Come on. You need some fresh air.

PAUL. Where are you taking me?

JOSEPH. The bench.

(JOSEPH *and* JULES *drag* PAUL *on to the verandah*)

PAUL. You're always sending me to that damn bench.

(JOSEPH *and* JULES *lead* PAUL *off on the verandah to* L. ALFRED *rises, removes his neckerchief, collects the cage and exits hurriedly down* L. *After a moment, the shop bell rings.*
      MARIE LOUISE *enters from the shop.*
      ALFRED *enters down* L)

MARIE LOUISE (*crossing to Alfred*) Oh, you're still here.

ALFRED. Yes.

MARIE LOUISE. Where's Paul?

ALFRED. Oh—here and there.

MARIE LOUISE. Is he—very upset?

ALFRED. Well—yes. I should say that Paul is very upset.

MARIE LOUISE. I met father coming out of church. He told me.

ALFRED. He told you?

MARIE LOUISE. Don't you know—about Uncle Gaston.

ALFRED. Oh, that one. Yes.

MARIE LOUISE. How awful.

ALFRED. I don't see why you should go into mourning—considering.

MARIE LOUISE. You don't understand. I said: how awful—because I should feel sorry, and I don't. Why are you staring at me?

ALFRED. I was just thinking of what you just said.

(JOSEPH *enters on the verandah from* L)

JOSEPH. Psst!

(JOSEPH *attracts* ALFRED'S *attention, and by a series of gestures indicates that Paul is dead and all is well. He then exits on the verandah to* L)

ALFRED. You know, you might think you're losing something, when you're really not. Sometimes you can be in love with something that doesn't even exist.

MARIE LOUISE. What are you hiding from me?

ALFRED. Well . . .

(JOSEPH *and* JULES *enter on the verandah from* L. *They stand for a moment, and take in the situation, then decide what to do and move to Marie Louise,* JOSEPH R *of her, and* JULES R *of Joseph*)

MARIE LOUISE. What's happened? Where's Paul? Are you trying to hint he—he doesn't love me? Is that it? Now that he's free, he doesn't want me. Is that it?

JOSEPH. He wants you—and loves you madly.

JULES. Even more than you love him.

JOSEPH. He said something to us this morning that we think you ought to know.

MARIE LOUISE. What?

JOSEPH. He said: "Gentlemen," he said, "my uncle's death has made me free to marry my darling Marie Louise, and only death can part us now."

MARIE LOUISE. He said that?

JULES. Even more eloquently.

JOSEPH. If that's conceivable. He said: and these were his very words—"She doesn't realize how shy I am. How can I tell her nothing in this world matters as much to me as her love—ambition? Wealth? Poof!"

JULES (*snapping his fingers*) "For her", he said, "I'd dig ditches —or . . ."

JOSEPH. "Or pick pockets."

JULES. Yes.

MARIE LOUISE. This is amazing. He's so reserved—generally —and he confided in *you.*

JOSEPH. The shock of his uncle's death—you know—he had to talk to someone.

MARIE LOUISE. And I wasn't here. Where is he?
JOSEPH. Well, as a matter of fact, he's in . . .
JULES. I think he's with your mother.
MARIE LOUISE. Excuse me . . .

(MARIE LOUISE *exits hurriedly by the arch up* L)

JOSEPH (*to Alfred*) Hey! Have you got Adolphe?
ALFRED. Yes, but what's the idea?
JULES (*crossing to* R *of the table and sitting*) It's a civilized custom to praise the dead, Alfred. It helps the living.
JOSEPH (*moving and sitting above the table*) We wanted to give her a memorial. She'll need one.

(ALFRED *crosses and sits* L *of the table*)

JULES. Let her at least cherish a memory.
JOSEPH. She's young. Someone'll come along. Someone always does.
JULES. It won't be you, Alfred, unfortunately. It could have been. It'll be someone else.
JOSEPH. The bell will ring—and there he'll be.
JULES. She won't love him as much as the mythical Paul—but she'll love him enough.

(*The shop bell rings. The* CONVICTS *rise.*
     FELIX *enters from the shop and hangs his hat on the hat-stand. The* CONVICTS, *disappointed, resume their seats*)

FELIX (*crossing to* C) What a time I've had. Please don't get up. The doctor'll be here soon.
JOSEPH. Good. He has his work cut out for him.
FELIX. My wife still in her room?
JULES. Yes.
FELIX. I thought last night I'd be spending an entirely different kind of Christmas. Life is strange.
JULES. Isn't it, m'sieu?
FELIX (*cheerfully*) Things work out somehow . . . (*He breaks off*) What am I saying? (*Guiltily*) I've got to see my wife.

(FELIX *exits by the arch up* L)

ALFRED (*rising*) Well—back to the roof.
JULES (*rising*) I suppose so.

(JULES *and* ALFRED *move up* C, *but are stopped by* JOSEPH)

JOSEPH. It's too much to ask Fate to send along the young man we're waiting for at this precise moment. Still, it would have been neater somehow. (*He rises*)

(*The* CONVICTS *move up* C *together. As they reach the verandah steps, the shop bell rings. They look at each other.
     SUB-LIEUTENANT ESPOIR, of the French Navy, enters from the*

shop. He is an extremely handsome young man in white naval uniform. The CONVICTS *stare at him as he moves above the table)*

(*He moves to* L *of the Lieutenant*) Yes?

LIEUTENANT. I beg your pardon, but there was no-one in the shop. This is M. Dulay's house, isn't it?

JULES (*moving to* R *of the Lieutenant*) It is.

(ALFRED *moves* LC)

LIEUTENANT. I suppose you work for him.

JOSEPH. We do, m'sieu.

LIEUTENANT. My ship docked last night and I should very much like to see M. Dulay.

JOSEPH. Oh, that'll be all right, won't it? Ooh, yes, will you kindly forgive one question—are you married?

LIEUTENANT. I beg your pardon?

ALFRED. Well, are you?

LIEUTENANT. No. Why?

JULES (*moving* R *of the table*) We were just wondering, m'sieu.

JOSEPH. You'll have to make certain allowances—have a little patience—you've chosen rather an awkward time to appear.

LIEUTENANT. Awkward?

JOSEPH. There's been a death or two in the house.

LIEUTENANT. Oh, I'm sorry to hear that.

JOSEPH. You needn't be sorry, m'sieu.

LIEUTENANT. Perhaps it would be better if I came back later.

(*He turns to go*)

CONVICTS (*together; closing in on him*) No!

JOSEPH. Oh, no, no. Don't move.

JULES. Life's too short. Take a seat, Lieutenant.

(*The* LIEUTENANT *removes his helmet and places it on the table.* ALFRED *sets out the chair* L *of the table.* JULES *and* JOSEPH *usher the Lieutenant to the chair*)

LIEUTENANT. But . . .

JOSEPH. Yes, do sit down, Lieutenant.

MARIE LOUISE (*off; calling*) M'sieu Joseph.

(JOSEPH *crosses to* L. ALFRED *moves down* L. JULES *stands above the table.*

MARIE LOUISE *enters by the arch up* L *and moves to* L *of Joseph. The* LIEUTENANT *moves behind Joseph, facing Marie Louise. As* JOSEPH *is between them,* MARIE LOUISE *cannot see the Lieutenant*)

M'sieu Joseph, why didn't you tell me Paul was in the garden? He's sitting out there on the bench. He looks as though he's fallen asleep, waiting for me.

(ALFRED *moves to the arch up* L)

JOSEPH. It's nice to know someone's waiting for you, m'selle.
(*He moves up* LC *and reveals the Lieutenant*)
MARIE LOUISE. Oh! Who's this gentleman?
JOSEPH. The future, m'selle.
LIEUTENANT (*crossing to Marie Louise*) Excuse me, are you
M'selle Dulay?
MARIE LOUISE. Yes.
LIEUTENANT (*saluting*) I am Lieutenant Espoir.

(MARIE LOUISE *curtsies*)

(*He takes a letter from his pocket*) I have a letter of introduction to
your father.
MARIE LOUISE. Oh, who from?
LIEUTENANT. From friends of his in Cherbourg.
MARIE LOUISE (*taking the letter from him*) Oh, he'll be delighted.
I'll take it to him, shall I?
LIEUTENANT. Thank you.
MARIE LOUISE. Won't you sit down?
LIEUTENANT. Thank you.

(MARIE LOUISE *turns and faces* ALFRED, *who moves down* L. *She
then exits by the arch up* L)

JULES. Now come along, Lieutenant, sit down, make yourself
at home.

(*The* LIEUTENANT *moves to the chair* L *of the table and sits*)

JOSEPH (*moving to* L *of the Lieutenant*) She's pretty, isn't she?
LIEUTENANT. She's charming.
ALFRED. Yes, she is.
JOSEPH. You're charming, too.
LIEUTENANT. What's that?
JOSEPH. You even look intelligent, which is more than we'd
hoped for.

(*The mouth-organ music is heard off*)

LIEUTENANT. Well, now, really. (*He makes a move to rise*)
JULES (*restraining the Lieutenant*) Now sit down. Relax. Close
your eyes. You've got nothing to do—except wait.
LIEUTENANT. If I closed my eyes, I'd be asleep in a minute. I
was up all night on the ship.
JOSEPH. Well, then, you sleep, Lieutenant. Sleep. Listen.

(*The music grows louder*)

There's your lullaby.

(*The* CONVICTS *back slowly up* C *and collect their hats*)

ALFRED. He doesn't know how lucky he is.

JOSEPH. And Marie Louise, she's found happiness and doesn't know it.

JULES. She's only seventeen. She doesn't realize that happiness wears many disguises.

ALFRED. Come, Adolphe. (*He collects the cage and starts up the ladder*)

JOSEPH. Well, Your Honour—(*he starts up the ladder*) didn't we have a wonderful Christmas?

JULES (*at the foot of the ladder*) Yes, we did.

JOSEPH. Let's do it again next year.

    The CONVICTS *exit up the ladder as—*

        the CURTAIN *falls*

FURNITURE AND PROPERTY PLOT

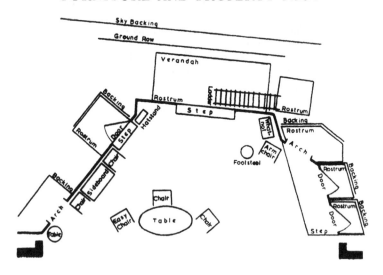

ACT 1

On stage—Dining-table. *On it:* red plush tablecloth, 3 ledgers, piles of loose
papers, bills and letters, bamboo fan

4 occasional chairs
Armless easy chair
Sideboard. *On it:* bowl of fruit (including banana), cruet, writing-pad,
knitting, cash-box with coins, pen, inkwell, candle-
stick with candle and matches, ornaments, oil lamp
In drawer: 6 knives, 5 forks, 5 spoons, 6 napkins, white
tablecloth
In cupboard: 6 glasses, 5 dinner-plates, 4 coffee-mugs,
3 cups, 3 saucers, 7 teaspoons
Occasional table (down R). *On it:* ornament
Hat-stand. *On it:* coat, Felix's panama hat
In corner up R: small crates, bales and boxes, box with small Christmas
tree, 3 strings of tinsel and 3 small angel dolls, bottle of cognac,
bottle of Beaujolais, corkscrew
On verandah: boxes, crates, roll of matting, Adolphe's coconut cage
In corner up L: crates and boxes, cardboard bottle crate. *In it:* bottle
of green Chartreuse
Victoria tapestry stand
High-backed wicker armchair
Footstool
Bamboo whatnot. *On it:* vase, account books, newspapers
Hanging shelves. *On them:* ornaments, vases
Oval carpet
On wall down R: barometer-thermometer

78

On walls: antlers, pictures, miniatures, mirror
In passage backing up L: stone jars, pictures
In kitchen backing down R: basket, small sack, kitchen utensils
Bamboo bead curtain
Red velvet swag border.
Lace curtain
2 bracket-type oil lamps
Pendant oil lamp

Off stage —Small block of wood, penknife (FELIX)
Tray. *On it:* bowl of oranges, squeezer, glass jug with lace and bead
cover (EMILIE)
Handful of small chicken feathers (JULES)
String bag. *In it:* pineapple (MME PAROLE)
Bunch of flowers (MARIE LOUISE)
Glass of water (ALFRED)
Pair of scissors, nail file (ALFRED)
Bottle of iodine (EMILIE)
White jacket on hanger (JOSEPH)
Wicker case (MARIE LOUISE)
Peignoir on hanger (JOSEPH)
Bamboo fan (JOSEPH)
Coins (JOSEPH)
Orchid, camellia (JULES)
Large decorated Christmas tree (JOSEPH)
Ring (JOSEPH)

Personal—FELIX: handkerchief
MME PAROLE: handbag. *In it:* 4 unopened letters
MARIE LOUISE: handbag. *In it:* note
JOSEPH: spectacles, large knife, coins

ACT II

Strike—Everything from table except plush cloth
From sideboard: glass of water, nail file, scissors, iodine, fan
Box and small tree
Wrapping paper
Vase of flowers from whatnot
Ornament from table down R

Set—Coconut cage by wicker chair up L.
Large tree on table down R
Account books and papers on sideboard
Bamboo fan on table C
Gaston's note on sideboard

Off stage—2 suitcases (PAUL)
Portfolio (GASTON)
Suit on hanger (PAUL)
Suitcase (JOSEPH)
Large sheet of cardboard, bamboo stick (JOSEPH)
Cigar (JOSEPH)
Plate with cold chicken wing (JULES)
Revolver (ALFRED)

Personal—ALFRED: coins

ACT III

Strike—Plate, candlestick, matches from table
       Graph card
       Dressing-gown
       Trousers only from suit on chair up L

Set—*On crates up* R: Joseph's hat
    On whatnot up L: Alfred's hat
    On hat-stand: Jules' hat
    On verandah by ladder: cage
    On wicker chair: bamboo pointer
    On table C: will, rough draft of will, Gaston's note
    On sideboard: tray. *On it:* jug of coffee, 3 mugs half filled with coffee, bowl
                         with lump sugar, jug of milk, 3 teaspoons in mugs

Off stage—Opened bottle of cognac (MME PAROLE)

Personal—MARIE LOUISE: handbag, prayer-book
       ALFRED: coin
       JULES: coin
       MME PAROLE: handbag. *In it:* 3 100-franc pieces
       PAUL: watch, handkerchief
       LIEUTENANT: letter

LIGHTING PLOT

Property Fittings Required—table oil lamp, 2 bracket-type oil lamps, pendant oil lamp (all practical)
  Interior. A living-room and verandah in the tropics. The same scene throughout
  THE MAIN ACTING AREAS COVER—the whole stage
  THE APPARENT SOURCE OF LIGHT IS—an open verandah back C

ACT   I   Late afternoon

To open: Effect of brilliant tropical sunshine

Cue 1   MARIE LOUISE: "What?"   (page 24)
  4-minute fade of lights, particularly on backcloth, as night falls

ACT   II   Night

  THE APPARENT SOURCES OF LIGHT ARE—an oil lamp on the sideboard R, an oil lamp on a beam up R, an oil lamp on a pole L, and an oil lamp hanging over the table C

To open: The stage in darkness except for moonlight and star effects on backcloth. All oil lamps dimmed until just in

Cue 2   JULES turns up lamp R   (page 29)
  Bring up lamp R and lights to cover area R

Cue 3   JULES turns up lamp up R   (page 29)
  Bring up lamp up R and lights to cover area C

Cue 4   JULES turns up lamp L   (page 29)
  Bring up lamp L and lights to cover area L

Cue 5   JOSEPH turns out lamp R   (page 53)
  Dim out lamp R
  Reduce lights R

Cue 6   ALFRED turns out lamp up R   (page 53)
  Dim out lamp up RC
  Reduce lights C

Cue 7   JULES turns out lamp L   (page 53)
  Dim out lamp L
  Reduce lights L

Cue 8   JOSEPH *lights candle*   (page 53)
  Bring in spot focused on Joseph and table

ACT III   Morning

To open: Effect of brilliant sunshine
           Lamps out

No cues

Lightning Source UK Ltd.
Milton Keynes UK
UKHW02f0118281117
313454UK00007B/424/P